Birds *of* Alaska
Field Guide

Stan Tekiela

PUBLICATIONS
Adventure
an imprint of AdventureKEEN

Acknowledgments

Special thanks to the National Wildlife Refuge System, which stewards the land that is critical to many bird species.

Edited by Sandy Livoti and Dan Downing

Cover, book design and illustrations by Jonathan Norberg

Range maps produced by Anthony Hertzel

Cover photo: Bald Eagle by Stan Tekiela

All photos by Stan Tekiela except p. 396 (female) by **Rick & Nora Bowers**; p. 40 (drying) by **Mike Danzenbaker**; pp. 330 (juvenile), 332 (juvenile) by **Dudley Edmondson**; pp. 46 (breeding male), 142 (winter), 260 (female), 282 (winter), 378 (in flight) by **Kevin T. Karlson**; pp. 98 (both), 252 (both) by **Gary Kramer**; pp. 44 (female), 50 (female), 78 (female & male), 82 (winter), 146 (winter), 158 (breeding), 288 (nonbreeding male), 290 (breeding), 380 (winter), by **Brian E. Small**; pp. 166 (both juveniles), 246 (Harlan's), 256 (juvenile perched), 326 (in-flight juvenile) by **Brian K. Wheeler**; and pp. 100 (both), 168 (Taiga), 242 (main), 304 (main), 308 (breeding), 322 (in flight), 328 (female), 334 (winter), 362 (main), 378 (breeding) by **Jim Zipp**.

Images used under license from Shutterstock.com
Agami Photo Agency: 34 (main), 56 (nonbreeding), 92 (male), 232 (male), 234 (male), 320 (in flight); **Bjorn Alards:** 86 (winter), 214 (winter); **Bouke Atema:** 36 (female), 236 (female); **Randy Bjorklund:** 182 (breeding female); **Leo Bucher:** 276 (male); **Maximillian Cabinet:** 388 (breeding); **Certhian Photography:** 92 (female), 234 (female); **Philippe Clement:** 370 (in flight); **Eric Dale:** 34 (female), 232 (female); **Erni:** 276 (female), 388 (winter); **Sophia Granchinho:** 288 (male); **Kerry Hargrove:** 182 (winter), 372 (winter); **Jukka Jantunen:** 62 (breeding male), 310 (breeding); **Piotr Krzeslak:** 274 (male); **Ivan Kuzmin:** 64 (breeding), 312 (breeding); **Wang LiQiang:** 184 (winter male), 374 (winter); **moosehenderson:** 388 (in flight); **Paul Reeves Photography:** 28 (nonbreeding), 84 (female), 216 (female); **Nick Pecker:** 68, 70, 82 (breeding), 146 (main); **Martin Pelanek:** 288 (female); **Piotr Poznan:** 370 (main); **RLHambley:** 28 (female), 294 (female); **rock ptarmigan:** 184 (breeding female); **Amit Satiya:** 28 (male), 294 (male); **Colin Seddon:** 84 (main), 216 (male); **Victor Slavgorodsky:** 274 (female); **Sandra Standbridge:** 80 (breeding); **Andrey V Vyalkov:** 402; **Greg A Wilson:** 272 (female); and **A Zargar:** 320 (main).

To the best of the publisher's knowledge, all photos were of live birds. Some were photographed in a controlled condition.

10 9 8 7 6 5 4 3 2 1

Birds of Alaska Field Guide
First Edition 2005
Second Edition 2023
Copyright © 2005 and 2023 by Stan Tekiela
Published by Adventure Publications
An imprint of AdventureKEEN
310 Garfield Street South
Cambridge, Minnesota 55008
(800) 678-7006
www.adventurepublications.net
All rights reserved
Printed in China
LCCN: 2022056412 (pbk); 2022056413 (ebook)
ISBN 978-1-64755-366-1 (pbk.); ISBN 978-1-64755-367-8 (ebook)

TABLE OF CONTENTS

WHAT'S NEW?

It is hard to believe that it's been more than 15 years since the debut of *Birds of Alaska Field Guide*. This critically acclaimed field guide has helped countless people identify and enjoy the birds that we love. Now, in this expanded second edition, *Birds of Alaska Field Guide* has many new and exciting changes and a fresh look, while retaining the same familiar, easy-to-use format.

To help you identify even more birds in Alaska, I have added 6 new species and more than 150 new color photographs. All of the range maps have been meticulously reviewed, and many updates have been made to reflect the ever-changing movements of the birds.

Everyone's favorite section, "Stan's Notes," has been expanded to include even more natural history information. "Compare" sections have been updated to help ensure that you correctly identify your bird, and additional feeder information has been added to help with bird feeding. I hope you will enjoy this great new edition as you continue to learn about and appreciate our Alaska birds!

WHY WATCH BIRDS IN ALASKA?

Millions of people have discovered bird feeding. Its a simple and enjoyable way to bring the beauty of birds closer to your home. Watching birds at your feeder often leads to a lifetime pursuit of bird identification. The *Birds of Alaska Field Guide* is for those who want to identify the common birds of Alaska.

There are over 1,100 species of birds found in North America. In Alaska alone there have been more than 530 different kinds of birds recorded throughout the years. These bird sightings were diligently recorded by hundreds of bird watchers and became part of the official state record. From these valuable records, I have chosen 156 of the most common and easily seen birds of Alaska to include in this field guide.

Bird watching, or birding, is one of the most popular activities in America. Its appeal in Alaska is due, in part, to an unusually rich and abundant birdlife. Why are there so many birds? One reason is open space. With more than 586,000 square miles (1,517,730 sq. km), Alaska is about one-fifth the size of the continental U.S. and is our largest state. From its farthest point east to its farthest point west, Alaska covers almost 1,500 miles (2,414 km), about the same distance as San Francisco to Minneapolis. Even if you were to divide Alaska in two, it would still rank first and second in size, with Texas coming in third. Alaska's total population, however, is only about 733,000 people. While this averages to just one person per square mile, most are located in four major cities in southern Alaska.

Open space is not the only reason there is such an abundance of birds in Alaska. Its also the diversity of habitat. Alaska has several mountain ranges—the Coast Range (includes the Kenai, Chugach, and Saint Elias Ranges), the Alaska Aleutian Range and Brooks Range. These ranges have 19 peaks higher than 14,000 feet (4,250 m), with Denali reaching 20,310 feet (6,190 m).

Mountainous regions are good places to see Boreal Chickadees and White-winged Crossbills.

Besides mountains, Alaska has over 27,000 glaciers, about 13 percent of all the glaciers in the world. It also has lush rain forests on the southern coast and dry sand dunes in the Arctic Circle.

Alaska has almost 45,000 square miles (117,000 sq. km) of tidal shoreline. Some areas have the greatest tidal variations in the world-up to 30 feet (9 m). The coastline of Alaska is longer than the coasts of all Lower 48 states combined. It includes the Aleutian Island chain, which is at least 1,000 miles (1,610 km) in length. Coasts are great places to see birds such as Common Eiders and Common Murres.

Fresh water also plays a large part in Alaska's bird populations. About three million lakes in the state are over 2 acres (.8 ha). Small lakes are wonderful places to see Red-necked Phalaropes and other birds. The largest lake, Lake Illiamna, covers around 1,000 square miles (2,600 sq. km). The Yukon River, the third longest river in the U.S., flows over 1,800 miles (2,900 km). Most rivers in Alaska are great places to see waterfowl such as Harlequin Ducks. Its always worth time to investigate bodies of water in Alaska for the presence of birds.

Varying habitats in Alaska also mean variations in the weather. Alaska's record temperatures range from a high of about 100 °F (38° C) to a low of -80° F (-62° C). Rainfall ranges from 2 inches (5 cm) annually in parts of the Arctic to over 300 inches (762 cm) in the rainforests of the southern coast. The weather is as diverse as the habitats in Alaska, making it one of the best places to see a wide variety of birds.

Wherever you go in Alaska, no matter if you're in the dry arctic tundra or moist mountains in southern parts of the state, there are birds to watch every season of the year. Whether witnessing the migration of hawks in fall or welcoming back shorebirds in spring, there is variety and excitement in birding as each season turns to the next.

OBSERVE WITH A STRATEGY: TIPS FOR IDENTIFYING BIRDS

Identifying birds isn't as difficult as you might think. By simply following a few basic strategies, you can increase your chances of successfully identifying most birds that you see. One of the first and easiest things to do when you see a new bird is to note **its color**. This field guide is organized by color, so simply turn to the right color section to find it.

Next, note the **size of the bird.** A strategy to quickly estimate size is to compare different birds. Pick a small, a medium and a large bird. Select an American Robin as the medium bird. Measured from bill tip to tail tip, a robin is 10 inches (25 cm). Now select two other birds, one smaller and one larger. Good choices are an American Tree Sparrow, at about 6 inches (15 cm), and an American Crow, around 18 inches (45 cm). When you see a species you don't know, you can now quickly ask yourself, "Is it larger than a sparrow but smaller than a robin?" When you look in your field guide to identify your bird, you would check the species that are roughly 6–10 inches (15–25 cm). This will help to narrow your choices.

Next, note the **size, shape and color of the bill.** Is it long or short, thick or thin, pointed or blunt, curved or straight? Seed-eating birds, such as Pine Grosbeaks, have bills that are thick and strong enough to crack even the toughest seeds. Birds that sip nectar, such as Rufous Hummingbirds, need long, thin bills to reach deep into flowers. Hawks and owls tear their prey with very sharp, curving bills. Sometimes, just noting the bill shape can help you decide whether the bird is a woodpecker, sparrow, grosbeak, blackbird or bird of prey.

Next, take a look around and note the **habitat** in which you see the bird. Is it wading in a saltwater marsh? Walking along a riverbank or on the beach? Soaring in the sky? Is it perched high in the trees or hopping along the forest floor? Because of diet and habitat preferences, you'll often see robins hopping on the ground but not usually eating seeds at a feeder. Or you'll see a Steller's Jay sitting on a tree branch but not climbing headfirst down the trunk, like a Red-breasted Nuthatch would.

Noticing **what the bird is eating** will give you another clue to help you identify the species. Feeding is a big part of any bird's life. Fully one-third of all bird activity revolves around searching for food, catching prey and eating. While birds don't always follow all the rules of their diet, you can make some general assumptions. Northern Flickers, for instance, feed on ants and other insects, so you wouldn't expect to see them visiting a seed feeder. Other birds, such as Tree and Cliff Swallows, eat flying insects and spend hours swooping and diving to catch a meal.

Sometimes you can identify a bird by **the way it perches.** Body posture can help you differentiate between an American Crow and a Red-tailed Hawk, for example. Crows lean forward over their feet on a branch, while hawks perch in a vertical position. Consider posture the next time you see an unidentified large bird in a tree.

Birds in flight are harder to identify, but noting the **wing size and shape** will help. Wing size is in direct proportion to body size, weight and type of flight. Wing shape determines whether the bird flies fast and with precision, or slowly and less precisely. Barn Swallows, for instance, have short, pointed wings that slice through the air, enabling swift, accurate flight. Rough-legged Hawks have long, broad wings for soaring on warm updrafts. Ruby-crowned Kinglets have short, rounded wings, helping them to flit through thick tangles of branches.

Some bird species have a unique **pattern of flight** that can help in identification. The American Crow flies with constantly flapping wings, while the Common Raven soars on out-stretched wings. Taking note of differences such as these can really help differentiate between similar-looking birds.

While it's not easy to make all of these observations in the short time you often have to watch a "mystery" bird, practicing these identification methods will greatly expand your birding skills. To further improve your skills, seek the guidance of a more experienced birder who can answer your questions on the spot.

BIRD BASICS

It's easier to identify birds and communicate about them if you know the names of the different parts of a bird. For instance, it's more effective to use the word "crest" to indicate the set of extra-long feathers on top of the head of a Steller's Jay than to try to describe it. The following illustration points out the basic parts of a bird. Because it is a composite of many birds, it shouldn't be confused with any actual bird.

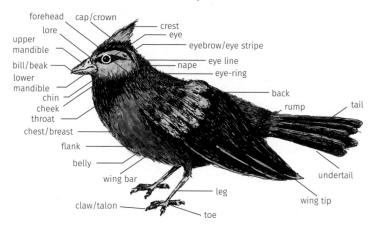

Bird Color Variables

No other animal has a color palette like a bird's. Brilliant blues, lemon yellows, showy reds and iridescent greens are common in the bird world. In general, male birds are more colorful than their female counterparts. This helps males attract a mate, essentially saying, "Hey, look at me!" Color calls attention to a male's health as well. The better the condition of his feathers, the better his food source, territory and potential for mating.

Male and female birds that don't look like each other are called sexually dimorphic, meaning "two forms." Dimorphic females often have a nondescript dull color, as seen in White-winged Crossbill. Muted tones help females hide during the weeks of motionless incubation and draw less attention to them when they're out feeding or taking a break from the rigors of raising the young.

The males of some species, such as the Downy Woodpecker, Steller's Jay and Bald Eagle, look nearly identical to the females. In woodpeckers, the sexes are differentiated by only a red mark, or sometimes a yellow mark. Depending on the species, the mark may be on top of the head, on the face or nape of neck, or just behind the bill.

During the first year, juvenile birds often look like their mothers. Since brightly colored feathers are used mainly for attracting a mate, young nonbreeding males don't have a need for colorful plumage. It's not until the first spring molt (or several years later, depending on the species) that young males obtain their breeding colors.

Both breeding and winter plumages are the result of molting. Molting is the process of dropping old, worn feathers and replacing them with new ones. All birds molt, typically twice a year, with the spring molt usually occurring in late winter. At this time, most birds produce their brighter breeding plumage, which lasts throughout the summer.

Winter plumage is the result of the late summer molt, which serves a couple of important functions. First, it adds feathers for warmth in the coming winter season. Second, in some species it produces feathers that tend to be drab in color, which helps to camouflage the birds and hide them from predators. The winter plumage of the male Common Loon, for example, is shades of gray, unlike its bold black-and-white pattern in summer. Luckily for us, some birds, such as the Steller's Jay, retain their bright summer colors all year long.

Bird Nests

Bird nests are a true feat of engineering. Imagine constructing a home that's strong enough to weather storms, large enough to hold your entire family, insulated enough to shelter them from cold and heat, and waterproof enough to keep out rain. Think about building it without blueprints or directions and using mainly your feet. Birds do this!

Before building, birds must select an appropriate site. In some species, such as the Wilson's Warbler, the male picks out several potential sites and assembles small twigs in each. The "extra" nests, called dummy nests, discourage other birds from using any nearby cavities for their nests. The male takes the female around and shows her the choices. After choosing her favorite, she finishes the construction.

In other species, such as the Varied Thrush, the female selects the site and builds the nest, while the male offers an occasional suggestion. Each bird species has its own nest-building routine that is strictly followed.

As you can see in these illustrations, birds build a wide variety of nest types.

| ground nest | platform nest | cup nest | pendulous nest | cavity nest |

Nesting material often consists of natural items found in the immediate area. Most nests consist of plant fibers (such as bark from grapevines), sticks, mud, dried grass, feathers, fur, or soft, fuzzy tufts from thistle. Some birds, including Rufous Hummingbirds, use spiderwebs to glue nest materials together.

Transportation of nesting material is limited to the amount a bird can hold or carry. Birds must make many trips afield to gather enough material to complete a nest. Most nests take four days or more, and hundreds, if not thousands, of trips to build.

A **ground nest** can be a mound of vegetation on the ground or in the water. It can also be just a simple, shallow depression scraped out in earth, stones or sand. Killdeer and Horned Larks scrape out ground nests without adding any nesting material.

The **platform nest** represents a much more complex type of construction. Typically built with twigs or sticks and branches, this nest forms a platform and has a depression in the center to nestle the eggs. Platform nests can be in trees; on balconies, cliffs, bridges, or man-made platforms; and even in flowerpots. They often provide space for the adventurous young and function as a landing platform for the parents.

Eurasian Collared-Doves don't anchor their platform nests to trees, so these can tumble from branches during high winds and storms. Hawks, eagles, ospreys and other birds construct sturdier platform nests with large sticks and branches.

Other platform nests are constructed on the ground with mud, grass and other vegetation from the area. Many waterfowl build platform nests on the ground near or in water. A **floating platform nest** moves with the water level, preventing the nest, eggs and birds from being flooded.

Three-quarters of all songbirds construct a **cup nest,** which is a modified platform nest. The supporting platform is built first and attached firmly to a tree, shrub, or rock ledge or the ground. Next, the sides are constructed with grass, small twigs, bark or leaves, which are woven together and often glued with mud for added strength. The inner cup can be lined with down feathers, animal fur or hair, or soft plant materials and is contoured last.

The **pendulous nest** is an unusual nest that looks like a sock hanging from a branch. Attached to the end of small branches of trees, this unique nest is inaccessible to most predators and often waves wildly in a breeze.

Woven tightly with plant fibers, the pendulous nest is strong and watertight and takes up to a week to build. A small opening at the top or on the side allows parents access to the grass-lined interior. More commonly used by tropical birds, this complex nest has also been mastered by kinglets. It must be one heck of a ride to be inside one of these nests during a windy spring thunderstorm!

The **cavity nest** is used by many species of birds, most notably woodpeckers and Mountain Bluebirds. A cavity nest is often excavated from a branch or tree trunk and offers shelter from storms, sun, cold and predators. A small entrance hole in a tree can lead to a nest chamber that is up to a safe 10 inches (25 cm) deep.

Typically made by woodpeckers, cavity nests are usually used only once by the builder. Nest cavities can be used for many subsequent years by such inhabitants as mergansers and bluebirds. Kingfishers, on the other hand, can dig a tunnel up to 4 feet (1 m) long in a riverbank. The nest chamber at the end of the tunnel is already well insulated, so it's usually only sparsely lined.

Who Builds the Nest?

Generally, the female bird constructs the nest. She gathers the materials and does the building, with an occasional visit from her mate to check on progress. In some species, both parents contribute equally to nest building. The male may forage for sticks, grass or mud, but it is the female that often fashions the nest. Only rarely does a male build a nest by himself.

Fledging

Fledging is the time between hatching and flight, or leaving the nest. Some species of birds are **precocial,** meaning they leave the nest within hours of hatching, though it may be weeks before they can fly. This is common in waterfowl and shorebirds.

Baby birds that hatch naked and blind need to stay in the nest for a few weeks (these birds are **altricial**). Baby birds that are still in the nest are **nestlings.** Until birds start to fly, they are called **fledglings.**

Why Birds Migrate

Why do so many species of birds migrate? The short answer is simple: food. Birds migrate to locations with abundant food, as it is easier to breed where there is food than where food is scarce. Orange-crowned Warbler, for instance, are **complete migrators** that fly from the tropics of Central and South America to nest in the forests of Alaska, where billions of newly hatched insects are available to feed to their young.

Other migrators, such as some birds of prey, migrate back to northern regions in spring. In these locations, they hunt mice, voles and other small rodents that are beginning to breed.

Complete migrators have a set time and pattern of migration. Every year at nearly the same time, they head to a specific wintering ground. Complete migrators may travel great distances, sometimes 15,000 miles (24,100 km) or more in one year.

Complete migration doesn't necessarily imply flying from the cold, frozen northland to a tropical destination. The Dark-eyed Junco, for example, is a complete migrator that flies back from the Lower 48 states and Canada to spend the summer right here in Alaska. This trip is still considered complete migration.

Complete migrators have many interesting aspects. In spring, males often leave a few weeks before the females, arriving early to scope out possibilities for nesting sites and food sources, and to begin to defend territories. The females arrive several weeks later. In many species, the females and their young leave earlier in the fall, often up to four weeks before the adult males.

Other species, such as the Red-necked Grebe, are **partial migrators**. These birds usually wait until their food supplies dwindle before flying south. Unlike complete migrators, partial migrators move only far enough south, or sometimes east and west, to find abundant food. In some years it might be only a few hundred miles, while in other years it can be as much as a thousand. This kind of migration, dependent on weather and the availability of food, is sometimes called seasonal movement.

Unlike the predictable complete migrators or partial migrators, **irruptive migrators** can move every third to fifth year or, in some cases, in consecutive years. These migrations are triggered when times are tough and food is scarce. Common Redpolls are irruptive migrators. They leave their normal northern range in search of more food or in response to overpopulation.

Many other birds don't migrate at all. Black-capped Chickadees, for example, are **non-migrators** that remain in their habitat all year long and just move around as necessary to find food.

How Do Birds Migrate?

One of the many secrets of migration is fat. While most people are fighting the ongoing battle of the bulge, birds intentionally gorge themselves to gain as much fat as possible without losing the ability to fly. Fat provides the greatest amount of energy per unit of weight. In the same way that your car needs gas, birds are propelled by fat and stall without it.

During long migratory flights, fat deposits are used up quickly, and birds need to stop to refuel. This is when backyard bird feeding stations and undeveloped, natural spaces around our towns and cities are especially important. Some birds require up to 2–3 days of constant feeding to build their fat reserves before continuing their seasonal trip.

Many birds, such as most eagles, hawks, Ospreys and falcons, migrate during the day. Larger birds can hold more body fat, go longer without eating and take longer to migrate. These birds glide along on rising columns of warm air, called thermals, that hold them aloft while they slowly make their way north or south. They generally rest at night and hunt early in the morning before the sun has a chance to warm the land and create good soaring conditions. Daytime migrators use a combination of landforms, rivers, and the rising and setting sun to guide them in the right direction.

The majority of small birds, called **passerines,** migrate at night. Studies show that some use the stars to navigate. Others use the setting sun, and still others, such as pigeons, use Earth's magnetic field to guide them north or south.

While flying at night may not seem like a good idea, it's actually safer. First, there are fewer avian predators hunting for birds at night. Second, night travel allows time during the day to find food in unfamiliar surroundings. Third, wind patterns at night tend to be flat, or laminar. Flat winds don't have the turbulence of daytime winds and can help push the smaller birds along.

HOW TO USE THIS GUIDE

To help you quickly and easily identify birds, this field guide is organized by color. Refer to the color key on the first page, note the color of the bird, and turn to that section. For example, the male Downy Woodpecker is black and white with a red mark on its head. Because the bird is mostly black-and-white, it will be found in the black-and-white section.

Each color section is also arranged by size, generally with the smaller birds first. Sections may also incorporate the average size in a range, which in some cases reflects size differences between male and female birds. Flip through the pages in the color section to find the bird. If you already know the name of the bird, check the index for the page number.

In some species, the male and female are very different in color. In others, the breeding and winter plumage colors differ. These species will have an inset photograph with a page reference and will be found in two color sections.

You will find a variety of information in the bird description sections. To learn more, turn to the sample on pp. 22–23.

Range Maps

Range maps are included for each bird. Colored areas indicate where the bird is frequently found. The colors represent the presence of a species during a specific season, not the density, or amount, of birds in the area. Green is used for summer, blue for winter, red for year-round, and yellow for migration.

While every effort has been made to depict accurate ranges, these are constantly in flux due to a variety of factors. Changing weather, habitat, species abundance and availability of vital resources, such as food and water, can affect the migration and movement of local populations, causing birds to be found in areas that are atypical for the species. So please use the maps as intended—as general guides only.

female
p. 405

male

Common Name

Scientific name **Color Indicator**

YEAR-ROUND
SUMMER
MIGRATION
WINTER

Size: measurement is from head to tip of tail; wingspan may be listed as well

Male: brief description of the male bird; may include breeding, winter or other plumages

Female: brief description of the female bird, which is sometimes different from the male

Juvenile: brief description of the juvenile bird, which often looks like the adult female

Nest: kind of nest the bird builds to raise its young; who builds it; number of broods per year

Eggs: number of eggs you might expect to see in a nest; color and marking

Incubation: average days the parents spend incubating the eggs; who does the incubation

Fledging: average days the young spend in the nest after hatching but before they leave the nest; who does the most "childcare" and feeding

Migration: type of migrator: complete (seasonal, consistent), partial (seasonal, destination varies), irruptive (unpredictable, depends on the food supply) or non-migrator

Food: what the bird eats most of the time (e.g., seeds, insects, fruit, nectar, small mammals, fish) and whether it typically comes to a bird feeder

Compare: notes about other birds that look similar and the pages on which they can be found; may include extra information to aid in identification

Stan's Notes: Interesting natural history information. This could be something to look or listen for or something to help positively identify the bird. Also includes remarkable features.

winter

breeding

European Starling
Sturnus vulgaris

YEAR-ROUND

Size: 7½" (19 cm)

Male: Glittering, iridescent purplish black in spring and summer; duller and speckled with white in fall and winter. Long, pointed, yellow bill in spring; gray in fall. Pointed wings. Short tail.

Female: same as male

Juvenile: similar to adults, with grayish-brown plumage and a streaked chest

Nest: cavity; male and female line cavity; 2 broods per year

Eggs: 4–6; bluish with brown markings

Incubation: 12–14 days; female and male incubate

Fledging: 18–20 days; female and male feed the young

Migration: partial to non-migrator; moves around to find food

Food: insects, seeds, fruit; visits seed or suet feeders

Compare: An urban bird that is not confused with other birds. Look for a long pointed bill and stubby tail to help identify. Usually seen in small to large flocks.

Stan's Notes: A great songster, this bird can mimic the songs of up to 20 bird species and imitates sounds, including the human voice. Jaws are more powerful when opening than when closing, enabling the bird to pry open crevices to find insects. Often displaces woodpeckers, chickadees and other cavity-nesting birds. Large families gather with blackbirds in the fall. Not a native bird; 100 starlings were introduced to New York City in 1890–91 from Europe. Bill changes color in spring and fall.

female
p. 163

male

SUMMER

Red-winged Blackbird
Agelaius phoeniceus

Size:	8½" (22 cm)
Male:	Jet black with red-and-yellow patches (epaulets) on upper wings. Pointed black bill.
Female:	heavily streaked brown with a pointed brown bill and white eyebrows
Juvenile:	same as female
Nest:	cup; female builds; 2–3 broods per year
Eggs:	3–4; bluish green with brown markings
Incubation:	10–12 days; female incubates
Fledging:	11–14 days; female and male feed the young
Migration:	complete, to western states
Food:	seeds, insects; visits seed and suet feeders
Compare:	Slightly smaller than Rusty Blackbird (p. 29). The bold red-and-yellow epaulets distinguish the male Red-winged from other blackbirds.

Stan's Notes: Summer resident in southeastern Alaska. Found around marshes, wetlands, lakes and rivers. Flocks with as many as 10,000 birds have been reported. Males arrive before the females and sing to defend their territory. The male repeats his call from the top of a cattail while showing off his red-and-yellow shoulder patches. The female chooses a mate and often builds her nest over shallow water in a thick stand of cattails. The male can be aggressive when defending the nest. Red-winged Blackbirds feed mostly on seeds in spring and fall, and insects throughout the summer.

female
p. 295

male

nonbreeding

SUMMER

Rusty Blackbird
Euphagus carolinus

Size: 9" (23 cm)

Male: Glossy black blackbird with blue and purple highlights. Bright yellow eyes. A short, thin pointed bill. Nonbreeding plumage is more rusty brown than glossy black.

Female: overall gray blackbird with rusty edges of feathers, yellow eyes, a short, thin pointed bill, nonbreeding is much browner with a gray rump and black patch around each eye

Juvenile: similar to female

Nest: cup; female builds; 1–2 broods per year

Eggs: 4–5; bluish with brown markings

Incubation: 12–14 days; female incubates

Fledging: 13–14 days; female and male feed young

Migration: complete, to the Lower 48 states

Food: insects, seeds

Compare: The male Red-winged Blackbird (p. 27) has red-and-yellow markings on its shoulders and is slightly smaller in size.

Stan's Notes: This bird nests across most of Alaska in small loose colonies, often preferring more wooded, swampy areas. Male feeds female while she incubates. Gathers in large groups. Flocks with other blackbirds to migrate in autumn. When in flight, the end of tail often appears squared.

in flight

YEAR-ROUND

American Crow
Corvus brachyrhynchos

Size:	16" (40 cm)
Male:	Completely black with a black bill, legs and feet. Can have a purple sheen in direct sun.
Female:	same as male
Juvenile:	similar to adult
Nest:	platform; female builds; 1 brood per year
Eggs:	4–5; pale blue with brown markings
Incubation:	16–20 days; female incubates
Fledging:	28–35 days; female and male feed young
Migration:	non-migrator; will move around in winter to find food
Food:	insects, fruit, seeds, fish, small mammals, carrion; comes to seed and ground feeders
Compare:	The American Crow is smaller than the Common Raven (p. 39), but lacks shaggy throat feathers and has a smaller bill and a lower pitched, more hoarse call.

Stan's Notes: One of the most recognizable birds in Alaska. Often reuses nest every year if not taken over by a hawk or owl. Can mimic other birds and human voices. One of the smartest birds and very social. Entertains itself by provoking chases with other birds and animals. Feeds on roadkill, but is rarely hit by cars. Cooperative hunting, with one crow sitting in a tree to watch for traffic while the other walks out to feed on the carrion. Extended families roost together at night in winter and communicate the location of food. In the morning the group flies to the food source. Unmated birds from the previous year help parents raise the current year's young. Can live 20 years.

Black Oystercatcher
Haematopus bachmani

YEAR-ROUND

Size: 18" (45 cm)

Male: An overall black body with a bright reddish orange, heavy straight bill. Yellow eyes with a red outline. Yellow legs and feet. Stocky body with a short tail and broad wings, as seen in flight.

Female: same as male

Juvenile: similar to adult, with light brown body and dull orange, black-tipped bill

Nest: ground; female and male construct; 1 brood per year

Eggs: 1–3; dull white to olive with brown marks

Incubation: 24–29 days; female incubates

Fledging: 35–40 days; female and male feed young

Migration: non-migrator to partial in Alaska

Food: insects, mollusks, worms, crustaceans

Compare: The breeding Black-bellied Plover (p. 65) has white on its head and a black and white back. Black Turnstone (p. 57) lacks yellow eyes outlined in red. Look for the stocky body and red-orange bill of Oystercatcher.

Stan's Notes: A shorebird found mainly along rocky shores. Rarely seen away from coast. Often alone and not approachable. Common name comes from its ability to feed on oysters and mussels. Uses its large bill to pry or sometimes chisel shells open with hammer-like blows. Believed to have a long-term pair bond. A noisy courtship display with much mutual bowing. Nest is a scrape on the ground, sometimes lined with shells and rocks, built above the high tide.

female p. 233

male

Black Scoter
Melanitta americana

SUMMER
WINTER

Size: 19¼" (49 cm)

Male: All-black duck with a large yellow knob at the base of bill and a narrow pointed tail.

Female: brown duck with a dark crown, pale white cheeks and thin dark bill

Juvenile: similar to female

Nest: ground; female builds; 1 brood per year

Eggs: 6–8; light pink to buff without markings

Incubation: 30–31 days; female incubates

Fledging: 45–50 days; female feeds young

Migration: partial migrator, to southern coastal Alaska, western coastal U.S. and Mexico

Food: mollusks, crustaceans, aquatic plants, seeds

Compare: Smaller than the male White-winged Scoter (p. 37), which has a white comma-shaped patch beneath each eye and a yellow and orange bill. Slightly smaller than male Surf Scoter (p. 93), which has a white patch on forehead and nape and a multicolored bill.

Stan's Notes: The least common of scoters, although once known as the Common Scoter. Often in mixed flocks numbering in the hundreds along the coast during migration and winter. Usually will feed in seawater 20–40 feet (6–12 m) deep, just outside the breaker zone. Nests on the tundra close to freshwater lakes and ponds, returning to sea after breeding season for the rest of the summer and winter. Female doesn't breed until her third summer. Male will leave female shortly after she starts to incubate. Broods sometimes gather in groups called creches and are tended by 1–3 older females.

female
p. 237

male

White-winged Scoter
Melanitta fusca

SUMMER
MIGRATION
WINTER

Size:	20½" (52 cm)
Male:	A black duck with a white comma-shaped patch underneath each eye. Large bicolored yellow and orange bill. Bright white eyes.
Female:	brown duck with a dark crown, large dull white patch just behind the eyes and at the base of a large dark bill
Juvenile:	similar to female
Nest:	ground; female builds; 1 brood per year
Eggs:	5–10; light pink to buff without markings
Incubation:	28–31 days; female incubates
Fledging:	50–60 days; female feeds young
Migration:	complete, to southern coastal Alaska, western coastal U.S. and Mexico
Food:	mollusks, crustaceans, aquatic insects and plants
Compare:	Larger than the male Black Scoter (p. 35), which lacks the white mark beneath each eye. Slightly larger than male Surf Scoter (p. 93), which has a multicolored bill and white patch on the forehead and nape.

Stan's Notes: Nests on the tundra in Alaska near freshwater lakes and ponds. Spends the winter at sea, rarely returning to shore. Sometimes in mixed flocks with other scoters. The genus name *Melanitta* from the Greek *melas* for "black" and *nitta* for "duck" describes the bird well. The common name was first used in the *Collective Catalogue of Birds* (1674), but its origins are unknown.

in flight

Common Raven
Corvus corax

YEAR-ROUND

Size: 22–27" (56–69 cm)

Male: Large all-black bird with a shaggy beard of feathers on throat and chin. Large black bill. Large wedge-shaped tail, best seen in flight.

Female: same as male

Juvenile: same as adult

Nest: platform; female and male construct; 1 brood per year

Eggs: 4–6; pale green with brown markings

Incubation: 18–21 days; female incubates

Fledging: 38–44 days; female and male feed the young

Migration: non-migrator; moves around to find food

Food: insects, fruit, small animals, carrion

Compare: American Crow (p. 31) is smaller, lacks the shaggy throat feathers and has a smaller bill and a lower pitched, more hoarse call. Glides on flat outstretched wings unlike the constant flapping of the American Crow.

Stan's Notes: Considered by some people to be the smartest of all birds. Known for its aerial acrobatics and long swooping dives. Soars on wind without flapping, like a raptor. Sometimes scavenges with crows and gulls. A cooperative hunter that often communicates the location of a good source of food to other ravens. Most start to breed at 3–4 years. Complex courtship includes grabbing bills, preening each other and cooing. Long-term pair bond. Uses the same nest site for many years.

drying

Pelagic Cormorant
Phalacrocorax pelagicus

YEAR-ROUND
SUMMER

Size: 28" (71 cm)

Male: A large black water bird that appears glossy green in direct sun. Long, snake-like white-washed neck. A long dark bill with a small orange patch at the base.

Female: same as male

Juvenile: similar to adult

Nest: platform, on a cliff in a colony; male and female build; 1 brood per year

Eggs: 3–5; light blue without markings

Incubation: 26–31 days; female and male incubate

Fledging: 37–45 days; female and male feed young

Migration: non-migrator to partial, to southern coastal Alaska

Food: small fish, aquatic insects

Compare: Smaller than the Double-crested Cormorant (p. 43), which has a larger gray bill with yellow at the base and a hooked tip.

Stan's Notes: Found exclusively around rocky ocean shores. Often seen flying low over the water's surface, moving from one rocky outcropping to another. Excellent vision in the air and underwater. Feeds mainly on fish, diving to depths over 100 feet (30 m). Nests on steep, rocky inaccessible cliffs for protection from predators. One mate will gather nesting material such as small sticks, seaweed and other debris, and the other builds. Uses the same nest each year, adding new material each season. Older nests can reach 5–6 feet (1.5–1.8 m) tall. Young hatch several days apart (asynchronously).

in flight

juvenile

crests

drying

YEAR-ROUND

Double-crested Cormorant
Phalacrocorax auritus

Size: 31–35" (79–89 cm); up to 4⅓' wingspan

Male: Large black waterbird with unusual blue eyes and a long, snake-like neck. Large gray bill, with yellow at the base and a hooked tip.

Female: same as male

Juvenile: lighter brown with a grayish chest and neck

Nest: platform; male and female construct; 1 brood per year

Eggs: 3–4; bluish white without markings

Incubation: 25–29 days; female and male incubate

Fledging: 37–42 days; male and female feed the young

Migration: non-migrator

Food: small fish, aquatic insects

Compare: Pelagic Cormorant (p. 41) is smaller, has a smaller bill and lacks the yellow patch at base of bill and the hooked tip.

Stan's Notes: Flocks fly in a large V or a line. Swims underwater to catch fish, holding its wings at its sides. This bird's outer feathers soak up water, but its body feathers don't. To dry off, it strikes an upright pose with wings outstretched, facing the sun. Gives grunts, pops and groans. Named "Double-crested" for the crests on its head, which are not often seen. "Cormorant" is a contraction from *corvus marinus*, meaning "crow" or "raven," and "of the sea."

male

female

Blackpoll Warbler
Setophaga striata

Size: 5½" (14 cm)

Male: Overall black and white with a distinctive black cap. White face below the eyes. Fine, vertical dark streaking on breast and flanks. Short dark bill. Short tail with white undertail. Yellow legs and feet.

Female: pale black and white, appearing gray with faint streaks on the breast and flanks, white undertail, yellow legs, lacks a black cap

Juvenile: similar to female, with a wash of pale yellow and a gray nape of neck

Nest: cup; female builds; 1 brood per year

Eggs: 3–5; white with brown markings

Incubation: 12–14 days; female incubates

Fledging: 11–12 days; female and male feed young

Migration: complete, to South America

Food: insects, seeds, berries

Compare: Northern Waterthrush (p. 137) and Arctic Warbler (p. 265) have a light stripe above eyes and lack the male Blackpoll's black cap.

Stan's Notes: A relatively large-bodied warbler that nests in spruce woods in Alaska. Builds nest near the trunk of a tree, where there is support from a horizontal branch. Usually a bulky nest of twigs, bark and grasses with a feather lining. A true migrant, making a roundtrip of up to 12,000 miles (19,000 km) to South America. Females return to the nesting area the following year and mate with the male in the nearest territory. Males molt in late summer and appear like females during autumn migration.

breeding male

winter male

female

Snow Bunting
Plectrophenax nivalis

Size: 7" (18 cm)

Male: Winter male has a white chin, breast and belly, and rusty brown head, back and shoulders. Small yellow bill. Black legs and feet. Breeding male is overall white with black-and-white wings.

Female: similar to breeding male, but lacks the all-white head

Juvenile: similar to winter male

Nest: cavity; female builds; 1–2 broods per year

Eggs: 4–7; green to blue with brown markings

Incubation: 10–16 days; female incubates

Fledging: 10–17 days; male and female feed young

Migration: partial to non-migrator in Alaska

Food: insects, seeds

Compare: This bird is easy to identify since no other small sparrow-like bird has so much white.

Stan's Notes: Seen throughout Alaska. Often feeds on the ground along roads. Usually seen in flocks of up to 30 individuals of mixed ages and sexes. Individual Snow Buntings appear slightly different from each other; some are completely black and white, others are a combination of black, white, brown and rust. Winter plumage is seen from September to March. Sometimes seen with other winter birds such as Horned Larks and Lapland Longspurs. Female constructs a grass and moss nest in a cavity or on a cliff that is well protected from the weather. Young hatch at different times, so some leave the nest before others.

male

female

YEAR-ROUND

Downy Woodpecker
Dryobates pubescens

Size: 6½" (15 cm)

Male: Small woodpecker with a white belly and black-and-white spotted wings. Red mark on the back of the head and a white stripe down the back. Short black bill.

Female: same as male but lacks the red mark

Juvenile: same as female, some with a red mark near the forehead

Nest: cavity with a round entrance hole; male and female excavate; 1 brood per year

Eggs: 3–5; white without markings

Incubation: 11–12 days; female incubates during the day, male incubates at night

Fledging: 20–25 days; male and female feed the young

Migration: non-migrator

Food: insects, seeds; visits seed and suet feeders

Compare: The Hairy Woodpecker (p. 53) is larger. Look for the Downy's shorter, thinner bill.

Stan's Notes: A year-round resident in parts of Alaska where trees are present. This is perhaps the most common woodpecker in the U.S. Stiff tail feathers help to brace it like a tripod as it clings to a tree. Like other woodpeckers, it has a long, barbed tongue to pull insects from tiny places. Mates drum on branches or hollow logs to announce territory, which is rarely larger than 5 acres (2 ha). Repeats a high-pitched "peek-peek" call. Nest cavity is wider at the bottom than at the top and is lined with fallen wood chips. Male performs most of the brooding. During winter, it will roost in a cavity. Doesn't breed in high elevations but often moves there in winter for food. Undulates in flight.

male

female

American Three-toed Woodpecker
Picoides dorsalis

YEAR-ROUND

Size: 8½" (22 cm)

Male: Mostly black with a white chin, breast and belly. Heavy black barring on the flanks and irregular white barring on back. Black line from base of bill to cheek. Yellow cap.

Female: similar to male, lacks a yellow cap

Juvenile: similar to male, often a larger yellow cap

Nest: cavity; female and male excavate; 1 brood per year

Eggs: 2–6; white without markings

Incubation: 12–14 days; female and male incubate, the female incubates during day; male at night

Fledging: 22–26 days; female and male feed young

Migration: non-migrator

Food: insects

Compare: The Black-backed Woodpecker (p. 55) is larger, with a well-defined yellow cap and a solid black back. Male Hairy Woodpecker (p. 53) is slightly larger and has a white stripe down the back and red mark on the back of head.

Stan's Notes: Was at one time considered the same species as the Black-backed Woodpecker. Most other woodpeckers have four toes on each foot, two forward and two rear. Lacks an inner rear-facing toe, resulting in three toes on each foot, hence its common name. Mated pairs may remain together year-round and mate for several consecutive years. Mates forage for food separately; usually low in trees. Nests in loose colonies, often near an abundant food source.

male

female

Hairy Woodpecker
Leuconotopicus villosus

YEAR-ROUND

Size: 9" (23 cm)

Male: Black-and-white woodpecker with a white belly. Black wings with rows of white spots. White stripe down the back. Long black bill. Red mark on the back of the head.

Female: same as male but lacks the red mark

Juvenile: grayer version of the female

Nest: cavity with an oval entrance hole; female and male excavate; 1 brood per year

Eggs: 3–6; white without markings

Incubation: 11–15 days; female incubates during the day, male incubates at night

Fledging: 28–30 days; male and female feed the young

Migration: non-migrator

Food: insects, nuts, seeds; comes to seed and suet feeders

Compare: Downy Woodpecker (p. 49) is much smaller and has a much shorter bill. Look for Hairy Woodpecker's long bill.

Stan's Notes: Found year-round in wooded areas in southeastern Alaska. Announces its arrival with a sharp chirp before landing on feeders. Responsible for eating many destructive forest insects. Uses its barbed tongue to extract insects from trees. Tiny, bristle-like feathers at the base of the bill protect the nostrils from wood dust. Drums on hollow logs, branches or stovepipes in spring to announce territory. Prefers to excavate nest cavities in live trees. Excavates a larger, more-oval-shaped entrance than the round entrance hole of the Downy Woodpecker. Makes short flights from tree to tree.

male

female

Black-backed Woodpecker
Picoides arcticus

YEAR-ROUND

Size: 9½" (24 cm)

Male: Mostly black with a white chin, breast and belly. Heavy black barring on flanks. Black line from base of bill to cheek. Yellow cap.

Female: similar to male, lacks a yellow cap

Juvenile: similar to male, often a larger yellow cap

Nest: cavity; male and female excavate; 1 brood per year

Eggs: 2–6; white without markings

Incubation: 12–14 days; female and male incubate

Fledging: 21–25 days; male and female feed the young

Migration: non-migrator

Food: insects

Compare: The American Three-toed Woodpecker (p. 51) has white barring on the back and a less defined yellow cap. The male Hairy Woodpecker (p. 53) is slightly smaller and has a white stripe down the back and a red mark on back of head.

Stan's Notes: Lacking an inner rear-facing toe, this bird is a close relative of the American Three-toed Woodpecker. Usually seen in recently dead trees from insect damage or fire. Named for its black back. Its white breast often becomes dark and sooty when feeding in a fire-damaged forest, making it appear all black. Feeds mainly on larvae of wood-boring beetles. Some estimate one woodpecker can eat more than 13,000 larvae annually. Species name *arcticus* is Greek for "near the bear" and refers to the Great Bear constellation in the northern sky and its northern range.

nonbreeding

Black Turnstone
Arenaria melanocephala

SUMMER
MIGRATION
WINTER

Size: 9½" (24 cm)

Male: Breeding (Apr–Aug) is overall black to dark gray with a white belly and white mark at base of bill. Short dark bill. Dark legs. Nonbreeding (Aug–Apr) lacks the white mark at base of bill.

Female: same as male

Juvenile: similar to nonbreeding adult, more gray

Nest: ground; male and female construct; 1 brood per year

Eggs: 3–4; yellow with brown markings

Incubation: 21–22 days; male and female incubate

Fledging: 18–20 days; female and male feed young

Migration: complete, to coastal Alaska

Food: aquatic insects; barnacles, mollusks, snails

Compare: Ruddy Turnstone (p. 59) has black and chestnut wings and a black and white head. Black Oystercatcher (p. 33) has yellow eyes outlined in red and a large red-orange bill.

Stan's Notes: Closely related to the Ruddy Turnstone. Seen mainly on rocky shores and beaches and, to a lesser degree, mud flats. The common name "Turnstone" comes from the habit of using its short, thick, slightly upturned bill to flip or turn over stones in search of food. Walks along rocky shores in a toylike fashion, seeming to be always on the move. Males will perform an aerial display during courtship. Nest is only a slight depression on the ground lined with dead grasses or mud, usually located close to water. Semi-colony nester, with both parents incubating eggs and brooding the young.

winter

breeding

Ruddy Turnstone
Arenaria interpres

Size: 9½" (24 cm)

Male: Breeding male has a white breast and belly with a black bib. Wings and back are black and chestnut. Head has a black-and-white marking. Orange legs. Slightly upturned black bill. Winter male has a brown-and-white head and breast pattern.

Female: similar to male but duller

Juvenile: similar to adults, but black-and-white head has a scaly appearance

Nest: ground; female builds; 1 brood per year

Eggs: 3–4; olive-green with dark markings

Incubation: 22–24 days; male and female incubate

Fledging: 19–21 days; male feeds the young

Migration: complete, to coastal California and Mexico

Food: aquatic insects, fish, mollusks, crustaceans, worms, eggs

Compare: Black Turnstone (p. 57) is overall black with dark legs. Look for orange legs and a bold pattern on head and neck to identify.

Stan's Notes: Summer resident and migrant in Alaska. Also known as Rock Plover. Named "Turnstone" because it turns stones over on rocky beaches to find food. Known for its unusual behavior of robbing and eating other birds' eggs. Hangs around crabbing operations to eat scraps from nets. Females often leave before their young leave the nest (fledge), resulting in males raising the young. Males have a bare spot on the belly (brood patch) to warm the young, something only females normally have.

Ancient Murrelet
Synthliboramphus antiquus

YEAR-ROUND WINTER

Size: 10" (25 cm)

Male: A small black and white bird with a very short, thick neck and tiny yellow-tipped bill. Black head and throat. Bright white on the neck. Distinctive white eyebrows.

Female: same as male

Juvenile: similar to adult, lacks white eyebrows and a black throat

Nest: cavity; male and female excavate; 1 brood per year

Eggs: 1–2; tan with brown markings

Incubation: 33–36 days; female and male incubate

Fledging: 35–40 days; male and female feed young

Migration: non-migrator; remains at sea except to nest

Food: aquatic insects, small fish

Compare: Smaller than the Common Murre (p. 81) which has a much larger, longer bill. Look for the white eyebrows to help identify.

Stan's Notes: Spends its time at sea (pelagic), coming to land only to nest each spring. Nests in large colonies in burrows under rocks and logs or in natural underground cavities. Breeding pair will dig a burrow down to 4 feet (1 m). Adults may mate for life, returning to the same nest burrow for many years. One parent will go out to sea to search for food, causing the other to incubate for up to 3 days nonstop before the mate returns. Parents switch incubating at night. Young leave the nest burrow at 2–3 days of age and move out to sea, using the cover of night to avoid predators such as gulls and falcons.

breeding
male

nonbreeding
p. 311

breeding
female

SUMMER MIGRATION

American Golden-Plover
Pluvialis dominica

Size: 11" (28 cm)

Male: Breeding (Apr–Sep) has a striking black face, neck, belly and undertail. Dark cap. White forehead with white extending to eyebrows and down the sides of neck. Dark back with golden highlights. Long dark legs and short black bill. Gray wing linings, seen in flight.

Female: similar to breeding male

Juvenile: similar to nonbreeding adult

Nest: ground; male builds; 1 brood per year

Eggs: 3–4; cream with brown markings

Incubation: 26–28 days; male and female incubate

Fledging: 20–22 days; male and female show young what to eat

Migration: complete, to South America

Food: insects, fruit, seeds

Compare: Similar size as breeding Black-bellied Plover (p. 65), which has a white undertail and rump. Look for the breeding American Golden-Plover's black undertail and dark cap to help identify. When it is in flight, also look for gray wing linings to help identify.

Stan's Notes: This bird was formerly called Lesser Golden-Plover. Was once hunted by market hunters. More than 48,000 birds were reported to have been shot in one day near New Orleans in 1861. Populations were extremely depleted by the early 1900s. May mate for life. Male does most of the nest selection and construction. Male also incubates most of the time. Both sexes feed the young equally.

winter
p. 313

breeding

Black-bellied Plover
Pluvialis squatarola

Size: 11–12" (28–30 cm)

Male: Striking black and white breeding plumage. Belly, breast, sides, face and neck are black. Cap, nape of neck, and belly near tail are white. Black legs and bill.

Female: less black on belly and breast than male

Juvenile: grayer than adults, with much less black

Nest: ground; male and female construct; 1 brood per year

Eggs: 3–4; pink or green with black-brown markings

Incubation: 26–27 days; male incubates during the day, female incubates at night

Fledging: 35–45 days; male feeds the young, the young learn quickly to feed themselves

Migration: complete, to coastal California and Mexico

Food: insects

Compare: Breeding Dunlin (p. 159) is slightly smaller, with a rusty back and long down-curved bill. Look for Black-bellied Plover's large black patch on the belly, face and chest, and a white cap.

Stan's Notes: Males perform a "butterfly" courtship flight to attract females. Breeds at age 3. Female leaves male and young about 12 days after the eggs hatch. Migrant and summer resident along coastal Alaska. During flight, in any plumage, displays a white rump and stripe on wings with black axillaries (armpits). Often darts across the ground to grab an insect and run.

female
p. 189

male

Bufflehead
Bucephala albeola

Size: 13–15" (33–38 cm)

Male: A small, striking duck with white sides and a black back. Greenish-purple head, iridescent in bright sun, with a large white head patch.

Female: brownish-gray with a dark-brown head and white cheek patch behind the eyes

Juvenile: similar to female

Nest: cavity; female lines an old woodpecker cavity; 1 brood per year

Eggs: 8–10; ivory-to-olive without markings

Incubation: 29–31 days; female incubates

Fledging: 50–55 days; female leads the young to food

Migration: complete, to southern coastal Alaska, western states, Mexico and Central America

Food: aquatic insects, crustaceans, mollusks

Compare: Look for the large white bonnet-like patch on a greenish-purple head to help identify the male Bufflehead.

Stan's Notes: A small, common diving duck, almost always seen in small groups or with other duck species on rivers, ponds and lakes. Most commonly found in sheltered bays and coastal harbors, it is also found inland on rivers and lakes. Nests in vacant woodpecker holes. Unlike other ducks, the young stay in the nest for up to two days before they venture out with their mothers. The female is very territorial and remains with the same mate for many years.

Horned Puffin
Fratercula corniculata

YEAR-ROUND
SUMMER

Size: 15" (38 cm)

Male: Large white and black head. Black back and wings. Enormous yellow bill with an orange tip. White chest, belly and underside of tail. Winter lacks a bold white and black pattern on head and has a dark bill with orange tip.

Female: same as male

Juvenile: similar to winter adult

Nest: cavity; male and female excavate; 1 brood per year

Eggs: 1; bluish white with gray markings

Incubation: 40–41 days; male and female incubate

Fledging: 40–45 days; male and female feed young

Migration: partial to non-migrator, along the West Coast from Alaska to Washington

Food: fish, aquatic insects, squid, mollusks, algae, urchins

Compare: Same size and similar shape as the Tufted Puffin (p. 71), which has a black belly and an enormous orange bill.

Stan's Notes: Colony nester on rocky islands with steep cliffs. Digs a burrow under a turf-covered slope down to 4 feet (1 m), ending in a nest chamber. Often silent; may give a low rumbling, groaning sound in colony. Usually flies up to 30 feet (9 m) above the water's surface; most other sea birds will fly only 5–10 feet (1.5–3 m) above the surface. A slow flier compared with other sea birds. Parents find food for their young, returning with many fish lined up in their bills. Parents locate offspring by their individual calls.

Tufted Puffin
Fratercula cirrhata

SUMMER

Size: 15" (38 cm)

Male: All-black body with a large white and black head and pale yellow feather tufts at back of head. An enormous orange bill. Winter lacks the bold white and black pattern on head and has a pale orange bill.

Female: same as male

Juvenile: similar to winter adult

Nest: cavity; male and female excavate; 1 brood per year

Eggs: 1; bluish white with gray markings

Incubation: 40–41 days; male and female incubate

Fledging: 40–45 days; male and female feed young

Migration: partial migrator along the West Coast from Alaska to Washington

Food: fish, aquatic insects, squid, mollusks, algae, urchins

Compare: Same size and similar shape as the Horned Puffin (p. 69), which has a white breast and belly and yellow at the base of bill.

Stan's Notes: Colony nester on rocky islands with steep cliffs. Digs a burrow under a turf-covered slope down to 8 feet (2 m), ending in a nesting chamber. Burrow is deeper than Horned Puffins, but otherwise the biology is very similar. A silent bird when away from the colony. While in colony; it may give a low rumbling, groaning sound. Usually seen flying up to 30 feet (9 m) above the water's surface; most other sea birds will fly only 5–10 feet (1.5–3 m) above the surface. A slow flier compared with other sea birds.

female p. 199

male

SUMMER MIGRATION

Lesser Scaup
Aythya affinis

Size: 16–17" (40–43 cm)

Male: Appears mostly black with bold white sides and a gray back. Chest and head look nearly black, but head appears purple with green highlights in direct sun. Bright-yellow eyes.

Female: overall brown with a dull-white patch at the base of a light-gray bill; yellow eyes

Juvenile: same as female

Nest: ground; female builds; 1 brood per year

Eggs: 8–14; olive-buff without markings

Incubation: 22–28 days; female incubates

Fledging: 45–50 days; female teaches the young to feed

Migration: complete, to western states and Mexico

Food: aquatic plants and insects

Compare: The male Greater Scaup (p. 85) has a more rounded head. Male Common Goldeneye (p. 91) has a white breast. The male Blue-winged Teal (p. 193) has a white mark at base of bill. Male Canvasback (p. 239) has a sloping forehead and long dark bill.

Stan's Notes: A common diving duck. Often seen in large flocks on lakes and ponds. Submerges completely to feed on the bottom (unlike dabbling ducks, which tip forward to reach the bottom). Frequently seen in large flocks numbering in the thousands on area lakes and ponds, and along the coast in winter. When seen in flight, note the bold white stripe under the wings. Interesting baby-sitting arrangement in which the young form groups tended by one to three adult females.

female
p. 201

male

Ring-necked Duck
Aythya collaris

SUMMER

Size:	16–19" (41–48 cm)
Male:	Striking black duck with light-gray-to-white sides. Blue bill with a bold white ring and a thinner ring at the base. Peaked head with a sloped forehead.
Female:	brown with darker-brown back and crown, light-brown sides, gray face, white eye-ring, white ring around the bill, and peaked head
Juvenile:	similar to female
Nest:	ground; female builds; 1 brood per year
Eggs:	8–10; olive-gray to brown without markings
Incubation:	26–27 days; female incubates
Fledging:	49–56 days; female teaches the young to feed
Migration:	complete, to southern states and Mexico
Food:	aquatic plants and insects
Compare:	Similar size as male Lesser Scaup (p. 73), which has a gray back unlike the black back of male Ring-necked Duck. Look for the blue bill with a bold white ring to identify the male Ring-necked Duck.

Stan's Notes: Usually in larger freshwater lakes rather than marshes, in small flocks or just pairs. Watch for this diving duck to dive underwater to forage for food. Springs up off the water to take flight. Flattens its crown when diving. Male gives a quick series of grating barks and grunts. Female gives high-pitched peeps. Named "Ring-necked" for its cinnamon collar, which is nearly impossible to see in the field. Also called Ring-billed Duck due to the white ring on its bill.

female
p. 203

male

SUMMER
MIGRATION

Harlequin Duck
Histrionicus histrionicus

Size: 17" (43 cm)

Male: Breeding is black and white with rusty red sides and top of head. Highest part of head just above the eyes. Small light-colored bill. Long pointed tail. Winter is overall brown with a white patch at sides of head and at base of bill. Faint white marks at shoulders and base of tail.

Female: similar to winter male

Juvenile: similar to female

Nest: ground; female builds; 1 brood per year

Eggs: 6–8; pale white without markings

Incubation: 28–31 days; female incubates

Fledging: 60–70 days; female leads young to food

Migration: complete migrator, to western states

Food: aquatic insects, crustaceans, mollusks

Compare: The male Greater Scaup (p. 85) and Lesser Scaup (p. 73) are similar in size, but have white sides. Look for the unique black and white pattern and rust sides to help identify.

Stan's Notes: A small duck that rides low in water. Found in fast-running rivers and streams, which presumably have a richer food supply than slow-moving water. Frequently walks in shallow water, foraging for food on the bottom among the rocks. Uses wings and feet to propel itself underwater unlike other diving ducks, which just use their feet. Female does not breed until 2 years of age. Male leaves female after she starts to incubate.

in flight

male

winter male

female

Long-tailed Duck
Clangula hyemalis

SUMMER
WINTER

Size: 17" (43 cm)

Male: Breeding (May–Oct) adult has a black head and neck and white face. Gray sides. Small dark bill with a tan ring. Very long, narrow tail. Winter (Nov–Apr) has a white neck and head with black and gray patches on face.

Female: overall brown with a dark face, white at the base of neck and around eyes, large white rump; winter has a white face and sides

Juvenile: similar to winter female

Nest: ground; female builds; 1 brood per year

Eggs: 6–8; pale green without markings

Incubation: 24–29 days; female incubates

Fledging: 35–40 days; female leads young to food

Migration: complete, to coastal Alaska and Canada

Food: aquatic insects

Compare: Breeding male Harlequin Duck (p. 77) has rusty red sides and a shorter tail.

Stan's Notes: Southern coastal duck in winter. Moves across Alaska in spring and summer to breed. Adults molt up to four times per year. Some molt continuously, but the males long tail is consistent and easily visible in flight. Fast fliers. Small groups fly just above the water's surface. One of the deepest diving ducks, diving down to 200 feet (60 m). Can stay submerged up to 1.5 minutes. Very vocal. The males have a yodeling call; females give soft calls and grunts. After hatching, young form groups (creches) that usually consist of 3–4 broods (10–30 individuals), but may have up to 100 ducklings. Older females often tend creches. Formerly called Oldsquaw.

breeding

winter

Common Murre

Uria aalge

YEAR-ROUND
SUMMER

Size: 17½" (44 cm)

Male: Breeding (Mar–Sep) has a dark brown-to-black head, neck, back and sides. Lower half is white. A long, slender, pointed black bill. Winter (Sep–Mar) has a white throat, chin and cheeks, with a narrow black stripe arching from behind eyes to sides of neck.

Female: same as male

Juvenile: similar to winter male

Nest: no nest; 1 brood per year

Eggs: 1; brown to olive (sometimes white) with brown markings

Incubation: 30–33 days; female and male incubate

Fledging: 19–25 days; male and female feed young

Migration: non-migrator to partial; moves away from northern Alaska in winter, farther out to sea

Food: small fish

Compare: Winter Thick-billed Murre (p. 83) lacks a narrow black stripe behind the eyes. The Ancient Murrelet (p. 61) has a tiny yellow tipped bill and a very short, stout neck.

Stan's Notes: A colony nester on cliffs, with colonies numbering in the thousands. Pairs return to the same nest spot each year. Moves a few pebbles to build nest. High-density nesters, some so close they touch. Incubates in semi-upright position, holding the egg with its feet. Pairs may mate for life. Nearly wiped out by the mid-1800s due to unregulated hunting. Populations now stable. Highly susceptible to oil spills. Bald Eagles seem to prefer these birds in their diet.

breeding

winter

Thick-billed Murre
Uria lomvia

YEAR-ROUND
SUMMER
WINTER

Size: 18" (45 cm)

Male: Breeding (Mar–Sep) has a dark brown-to-black head, neck, back and sides. Lower half is white. A long, thick, pointed black bill, slightly down-curved at the tip. Winter (Sep–Mar) has a white throat and chin.

Female: same as male

Juvenile: similar to winter adult, but has a black and white speckled throat and chin

Nest: no nest; 1 brood per year

Eggs: 1; light blue to olive (sometimes white) with brown markings

Incubation: 30–35 days; female and male incubate

Fledging: 19–25 days; male and female feed young

Migration: non-migrator to partial; moves away from northern Alaska in winter, farther out to sea

Food: small fish

Compare: The winter Common Murre (p. 81) has a narrow black stripe behind the eyes. The Ancient Murrelet (p. 61) has a tiny yellow tipped bill and a very short, stout neck.

Stan's Notes: Breeds on cliffs in very large colonies of over 10,000 pairs. Only 11 colonies compose nearly all of the breeding Thick-billed Murres. Adults mate for life, but are more likely committed to the nest site rather than to each other. Female incubates during the day; male mainly at night. Incubates egg by continuously pressing it against brood patch with its feet. After hatching, male tends young for several weeks. Many are killed each year in oil spills and fish nets.

female
p. 217

male

Greater Scaup
Aythya marila

Size: 18" (45 cm)

YEAR-ROUND
SUMMER
MIGRATION
WINTER

Male: A mostly black and white duck. Black head shines green in direct sunlight. Bright white sides and a gray back. Light blue bill with a black tip. Rounded head.

Female: brown with a darker head and a bold white patch at the base of bill, might show a white patch behind each eye, rounded top of head

Juvenile: same as female

Nest: ground; female builds; 1 brood per year

Eggs: 7–10; greenish olive without markings

Incubation: 24–28 days; female incubates

Fledging: 45–50 days; female teaches young to feed

Migration: complete to non-migrator, to western coastal U.S., Mexico

Food: aquatic plants and insects

Compare: The male Lesser Scaup (p. 73) is very similar, but male Greater Scaup is slightly larger, has a more rounded head and a larger black mark on the tip of bill. The male Common Goldeneye (p. 91) has a white chest and a distinctive white mark in front of each eye. The male Canvasback (p. 367) is larger and has a red head and neck.

Stan's Notes: Common summer resident and migrant, breeding in the southern two-thirds of Alaska. More common than the Lesser Scaup, but before 1920, the Lesser Scaup was more common. Most abundant on large saltwater bays.

winter
p. 215

breeding

Red-necked Grebe
Podiceps grisegena

YEAR-ROUND
SUMMER
MIGRATION
WINTER

Size: 18" (45 cm)

Male: Breeding (Feb-Aug) has a bold black and white pattern on the head, a rusty red neck and brown body. Long thin bill with yellow lower mandible and dark upper.

Female: same as male

Juvenile: similar to winter adult

Nest: floating platform; female and male build; 1 brood per year

Eggs: 3–6; white without markings

Incubation: 21–23 days; female and male incubate

Fledging: 50–70 days; female and male feed young

Migration: complete to non-migrator in Alaska

Food: aquatic insects, small fish

Compare: The breeding Common Loon (p. 103) has a checkered back. Breeding Common Murre (p. 81) has a dark head and neck.

Stan's Notes: One of seven grebe species in North America. Like the other grebes, it has a tiny tail that is usually hidden in its fluffy feathers at the base of tail (coverts). It has lobed toes unlike ducks, which have webbed feet. Found in small ponds and shallow lakes lined with reeds and sedges. Forages for food by diving for aquatic insects, often remaining underwater for up to a minute. Doesn't fly much once at nesting grounds. Builds a floating nest with plants and anchors it to one spot. Floating keeps nest from submerging when water rises during spring snowmelt. Young hatch one day at a time. Parents feed the young tiny feathers. This presumably helps protect the stomach lining from bones in fish, its main diet.

female
p. 221

male

Barrow's Goldeneye
Bucephala islandica

SUMMER
WINTER

Size: 18–20" (45–50 cm)

Male: A black and white duck with a large puffy head. Head appears deep green in bright sunlight. Top of head is low and flat. Bright golden eyes. A large crescent-shaped white mark in front of each eye. Small dark bill.

Female: large dark brown head, gray body, golden eyes, small mostly yellow bill, white collar

Juvenile: same as female, but has a dark bill

Nest: cavity; female lines old woodpecker cavity; 1 brood per year

Eggs: 9–11; green to olive without markings

Incubation: 32–34 days; female incubates

Fledging: 55–60 days; female leads young to food

Migration: partial migrator, to southern coastal Alaska and western coastal states

Food: aquatic insects and plants, mollusks

Compare: Male Common Goldeneye (p. 91) has a round white spot in front of each eye and a tall, almost peaked top of head. Look for a white crescent mark in front of each eye.

Stan's Notes: Nests in cavities near ponds and lakes. Will also use a nest box. Female often returns to the same nest location for many years. Female may mate with the same male from year to year. Male leaves female once she starts incubating. Nestlings leave the nest in just 24–36 hours. Often swims out to open water when threatened instead of flying away. Will hybridize with the closely related Common Goldeneye, producing a bird with a maroon head.

female
p. 223

male

Common Goldeneye
Bucephala clangula

SUMMER
WINTER

Size: 18–20" (45–51 cm)

Male: Mostly white duck with a black back and a large, puffy, green head. Large white spot on the face. Bright-golden eyes. Dark bill.

Female: large dark-brown head with a gray body and a white collar, bright-golden eyes, yellow-tipped dark bill

Juvenile: same as female but has dark eyes

Nest: cavity; female lines an old woodpecker cavity; 1 brood per year

Eggs: 8–10; light green without markings

Incubation: 28–32 days; female incubates

Fledging: 56–59 days; female leads the young to food

Migration: complete, to southern coastal Alaska, western states and Mexico

Food: aquatic plants, insects, fish, mollusks

Compare: The male Barrow's Goldeneye (p. 89) has a white crescent mark in front of each eye. The male Greater Scaup (p. 85) and Lesser Scaup (p. 73) are similar, but smaller. Look for the white chest and round white spot in front of each golden eye.

Stan's Notes: Known for the loud whistling sound produced by its wings during flight. During late winter and early spring, the male performs elaborate mating displays that include throwing his head back and calling a raspy note. The female will lay some of her eggs in other goldeneye nests or in the nests of other species (called egg dumping), causing some mothers to incubate as many as 30 eggs in a brood. Named for its bright-golden eyes.

in flight

male

female
p. 235

Surf Scoter
Melanitta perspicillata

SUMMER
MIGRATION
WINTER

Size: 20" (51 cm)

Male: Black duck with a white patch on forehead and nape of neck. Large multicolored bill a white base, black spot and orange tip. Bright white eyes.

Female: brown duck with a dark crown, white mark on nape, vertical white patch at the base of a large dark bill

Juvenile: similar to female

Nest: ground; female builds; 1 brood per year

Eggs: 5–8; light pink to buff without markings

Incubation: 30–31 days; female incubates

Fledging: 45–50 days; female feeds young

Migration: partial to complete, to southern coastal Alaska, western coastal U.S. and Mexico

Food: mollusks, crustaceans, aquatic insects

Compare: Male Black Scoter (p. 35) has a yellow knob on its bill and lacks white patches on head. Male White-winged Scoter (p. 37) has a white patch underneath each eye and a smaller, bicolored yellow and orange bill.

Stan's Notes: Dives or scoots through breaking surf. However, the common name "Scoter" may refer to the sooty black color of its plumage. Dives down to 40 feet (12 m) in seawater, foraging for mussels and crustaceans. Fish eggs make up 90 percent of its diet during spring and early summer. Nests on the tundra in Alaska near freshwater lakes and ponds. Spends the winter at sea, rarely returning to shore. Sometimes in mixed flocks with other scoters.

Black-billed Magpie
Pica hudsonia

YEAR-ROUND

Size: 20" (50 cm)

Male: Large black-and-white bird with a very long tail and white belly. Iridescent green wings and tail in direct sunlight. Large black bill and legs. White wing patches flash in flight.

Female: same as male

Juvenile: same as adult, but has a shorter tail

Nest: modified pendulous; male and female build; 1 brood per year

Eggs: 5–8; green with brown markings

Incubation: 16–21 days; female incubates

Fledging: 25–29 days; female and male feed young

Migration: non-migrator; moves around to find food

Food: insects, carrion, fruit, seeds

Compare: Contrasting black-and-white colors and the very long tail of Magpie distinguish it from the all-black American Crow (p. 31).

Stan's Notes: A wonderfully intelligent bird that is able to mimic dogs, cats and even people. Will often raid a barnyard dog dish for food. Feeds on a variety of food from roadkill to insects and seeds it collects from the ground. Easily identified by its bold black-and-white colors and long streaming tail. Travels in small flocks, usually family members, and tends to be very gregarious. Breeds in small colonies. Unusual dome nest (dome-shaped roof) deep within thick shrubs. Mates with same mate for several years. Prefers open fields with cattle or sheep, where it feeds on insects attracted to livestock.

soaring

Osprey
Pandion haliaetus

SUMMER

Size: 21–24" (53–61 cm); up to 5½' wingspan

Male: Large eagle-like bird with a white chest, belly and head. Dark eye line. Nearly black back. Black "wrist" marks on the wings. Dark bill.

Female: same as male but slightly larger and with a necklace of brown streaks

Juvenile: similar to adults, with a light-tan breast

Nest: platform on a raised wooden platform, man-made tower or tall dead tree; female and male build; 1 brood per year

Eggs: 2–4; white with brown markings

Incubation: 32–42 days; female and male incubate

Fledging: 48–58 days; male and female feed the young

Migration: complete, to southern states, Mexico and Central and South America

Food: fish

Compare: The juvenile Bald Eagle (p. 105) is brown with white speckles. The adult Bald Eagle has an all-white head and tail. Look for the white belly and dark eye line to identify the Osprey.

Stan's Notes: The only species in its family, and the only raptor that plunges into water feet first to catch fish. Always near water. Can hover for a few seconds before diving. Carries fish in a head-first position for better aerodynamics. Wings angle back in flight. Often harassed by Bald Eagles for its catch. Gives a high-pitched, whistle-like call, often calling in flight as a warning. Mates have a long-term pair bond. May not migrate to the same wintering grounds. Was nearly extinct but is now doing well.

female
p. 253

male

Common Eider
Somateria mollissima

YEAR-ROUND
SUMMER
WINTER

Size: 24" (60 cm)

Male: Black and white duck with a large body and short neck. Long forehead slopes into a large yellow bill. Black cap, concealing dark eyes. Often has a green wash to nape of neck.

Female: smaller than male, brown with a gray bill

Juvenile: similar to female

Nest: ground; female builds; 1 brood per year

Eggs: 3–6; pale green without markings

Incubation: 25–30 days; female incubates

Fledging: 65–75 days; female leads young to food

Migration: partial to non-migrator

Food: aquatic insects

Compare: The large size, unique shape and forehead sloping into a large yellow bill make this duck easy to identify: Look for a heavy body and broad wings during flight.

Stan's Notes: This is our largest sea duck. Found along the Pacific and Atlantic Coasts. The western Arctic variety has a yellow bill, while the eastern variety has a green bill. Nests in small colonies on tundra ponds and rocky shores, usually within 100 feet (30 m) of water. Often prefers to nest on small islands that lack mammalian populations, especially Arctic Foxes. Mates may stay together for several years, but the male will leave the female shortly after she begins to incubate. Mothers usually don't eat while incubating, but leave to feed, regaining lost body fat after the young fledge. Two or three groups of ducklings gathered together (creches) are tended by 1–2 older females.

in flight

Brant

Branta bernicla

Size: 25" (63 cm); up to 3½' wingspan

Male: A large black and white goose. Black head and neck with a small white necklace just under the chin. Small dark bill. Belly ranges from light gray to black. White rump and tail. Black edge of tail. Black legs and feet.

Female: same as male

Juvenile: similar to adult by its first summer

Nest: ground; female builds; 1 brood per year

Eggs: 4–8; pale white without markings

Incubation: 22–26 days; female incubates

Fledging: 40–50 days; female and male lead the young to food

Migration: partial migrator to complete, to western coastal U.S., Mexico

Food: aquatic insects, grasses, sedges, moss, seeds, lichen

Compare: Smaller than Greater White-fronted Goose (p. 255), which lacks the dark head, neck and white necklace. Similar size as Canada Goose (p. 339), which has a white cheek patch. Look for the Brant's white necklace.

Stan's Notes: A coastal goose, almost always in flocks on shallow bays, river deltas and marshes. Flocks fly in irregular V shapes with other goose species. Nearly half nest on the Yukon-Kuskokwim Delta; the rest nest farther north along coastal Alaska. Usually nests in shallow depressions lined with seaweed and down from mother. Mother covers her eggs with downy feathers when not incubating.

winter

breeding

Common Loon
Gavia immer

Size: 28–36" (71–91 cm)

Male: Checkerboard back, black head, white necklace. Deep-red eyes. Long, pointed black bill.
Winter plumage has a gray body and bill.

Female: same as male

Juvenile: similar to winter plumage, but lacks red eyes

Nest: ground, usually at the shoreline; female and
male build; 1 brood per year

Eggs: 2; olive-brown, occasionally brown markings

Incubation: 26–31 days; female and male incubate

Fledging: 75–80 days; female and male feed the young

Migration: complete to non-migrator in Alaska

Food: fish, aquatic insects, crayfish, salamanders

Compare: The breeding Red-throated Loon (p. 335) has
a red throat. Double-crested Cormorant (p. 43)
has a black chest and gray bill with yellow at
the base and a hooked tip.

Stan's Notes: A true symbol of the wildness of our lakes. Hunts for
fish by eyesight and prefers clear, clean lakes. A great swimmer,
but its legs are set so far back that it has a hard time walking.
"Loon" comes from the Scandinavian term *lom*, meaning "lame,"
for the awkward way it walks on land. Its wailing call suggests
wild laughter, which led to the phrase "crazy as a loon." Also gives
soft hoots. In the water, young ride on the backs of their parents
for about 10 days. Adults perform distraction displays to protect
the young. Very sensitive to disturbance during nesting and will
abandon the nest.

soaring

juvenile

soaring
juvenile

YEAR-ROUND
SUMMER

Bald Eagle
Haliaeetus leucocephalus

Size: 31–37" (79–94 cm); up to 7½' wingspan

Male: White head and tail contrast sharply with the dark-brown-to-black body and wings. Large, curved yellow bill and yellow feet.

Female: same as male but larger

Juvenile: dark brown with white speckles and spots on the body and wings; gray bill

Nest: massive platform, usually in a tree; female and male build; 1 brood per year

Eggs: 2–3; off-white without markings

Incubation: 34–36 days; female and male incubate

Fledging: 75–90 days; female and male feed the young

Migration: partial to non-migrator; will move around to find food

Food: fish, carrion, birds (mainly ducks)

Compare: The Golden Eagle (p. 257) lacks the white head and white tail of adult Bald Eagle. The juvenile Golden Eagle, with its white wrist marks and white base of tail, is similar to the juvenile Bald Eagle.

Stan's Notes: Nearly became extinct due to DDT poisoning and illegal killing. Returns to the same nest each year, adding more sticks and enlarging it to huge proportions, at times up to 1,000 pounds (450 kg). In their midair mating ritual, one eagle flips upside down and locks talons with another. Both tumble, then break apart to continue flight. Not uncommon for juveniles to perform this mating ritual even though they have not reached breeding age. Long-term pair bond but will switch mates when not successful at reproducing. Juveniles attain the white head and tail at 4–5 years of age.

Tree Swallow
Tachycineta bicolor

Size: 5–6" (13–15 cm)

Male: Blue-green in spring, greener in fall. Changes color in direct sunlight. White from chin to belly. Long, pointed wing tips. Notched tail.

Female: similar to male but duller

Juvenile: gray brown with a white belly and a grayish breast band

Nest: cavity; female and male line a vacant woodpecker cavity or nest box; 2 broods per year

Eggs: 4–6; white without markings

Incubation: 13–16 days; female incubates

Fledging: 20–24 days; female and male feed the young

Migration: complete, to Mexico and Central America

Food: insects

Compare: The Barn Swallow (p. 109) has a rust belly and deeply forked tail. The Bank Swallow (p. 125) has a breast band and lacks the Tree Swallow's iridescent blue green colors. The Cliff Swallow (p. 127) is a similar size and has a unique tan-to-rust color pattern.

Stan's Notes: The first swallow species to return each spring. Most common along ponds, lakes and agricultural fields. Can be attracted to your yard with a nest box. Competes with bluebirds for cavities and nest boxes. Builds a grass nest within and will travel long distances, looking for dropped feathers for the lining. Watch for it playing and chasing after feathers. Flies with rapid wingbeats, then glides. Gives a series of gurgles and chirps. Chatters when upset or threatened. Eats many nuisance bugs. Gathers in large flocks to migrate.

SUMMER

Barn Swallow
Hirundo rustica

Size: 7" (18 cm)

Male: Sleek swallow. Blue-black back, cinnamon belly and reddish-brown chin. White spots on a long, deeply forked tail.

Female: same as male but with a whitish belly

Juvenile: similar to adults, with a tan belly and chin, and shorter tail

Nest: cup; female and male build; 2 broods per year

Eggs: 4–5; white with brown markings

Incubation: 13–17 days; female incubates

Fledging: 18–23 days; female and male feed the young

Migration: complete, to South America

Food: insects (prefers beetles, wasps, flies)

Compare: The Tree Swallow (p. 107) has a white belly and chin and a notched tail. Bank Swallow (p. 125) lacks the cinnamon belly and blue black back. The Cliff Swallow (p. 127) and Violet-green Swallow (p. 343) are smaller and lack the distinctive, deeply forked tail. Violet-green Swallow has a white face.

Stan's Notes: Of the five swallow species regularly found in Alaska, this is the only one with a deeply forked tail. Unlike other swallows, it rarely glides in flight. Usually flies low over land or water. Drinks as it flies, skimming water, or will sip water droplets on wet leaves. Bathes while flying through rain or sprinklers. Gives a twittering warble, followed by a mechanical sound. Builds a mud nest with up to 1,000 beak-loads of mud. Nests on barns and houses, under bridges and in other sheltered places. Often nests in colonies of 4–6 birds; sometimes nests alone.

male

female

Mountain Bluebird
Sialia currucoides

SUMMER
MIGRATION

Size: 7" (18 cm)

Male: Overall sky-blue bird with a darker blue head, back, wings and tail. White lower belly. Thin black bill.

Female: similar to male, but paler with a nearly gray head and chest and a whitish belly

Juvenile: similar to adult of the same sex

Nest: cavity, old woodpecker cavity, wooden nest box; female builds; 1–2 broods per year

Eggs: 4–6; pale blue without markings

Incubation: 13–14 days; female incubates

Fledging: 22–23 days; female and male feed young

Migration: complete, to southwestern states and Mexico

Food: insects, fruit

Compare: Larger than Bluethroat (p. 275), which is gray with blue only around the area of the throat. Look for male Mountain Bluebird's dark blue head, back and wings.

Stan's Notes: Common in open mountainous country. Main diet is insects but will also eat fruit. Often hovers just before diving to the ground to grab an insect. Due to conservation of suitable nesting sites (dead trees with cavities and man-made nest boxes), populations have increased dramatically. Like other bluebirds, Mountain Bluebirds take well to nest boxes and tolerate close contact with people. Female sits on baby birds (brood) for up to six days after the eggs hatch. Young imprint on their first nest box or cavity and then choose a similar type of box or cavity throughout their life.

YEAR-ROUND

Steller's Jay
Cyanocitta stelleri

Size: 11" (28 cm)

Male: Dark-blue wings, tail and belly. Black head, nape and chest. Large, pointed black crest on head that can be lifted at will.

Female: same as male

Juvenile: similar to adult

Nest: cup; female and male construct; 1 brood per year

Eggs: 3–5; pale green with brown markings

Incubation: 14–16 days; female incubates

Fledging: 16–18 days; female and male feed the young

Migration: non-migrator; moves around to find food

Food: insects, berries, seeds; will visit seed feeders

Compare: The Canada Jay (p. 315) is slightly larger and lacks any blue and a crest. Belted Kingfisher (p. 115) is larger, lacks the black head and has a less prominent crest.

Stan's Notes: A year-round resident of foothills and lower mountains in southeastern Alaska. Thought to mate for life, rarely dispersing far, usually breeding within 10 miles (16 km) of birthplace. Several subspecies found throughout the West. The Alaska form (shown) has a black crest and lacks any distinct white streaks on head. Usually very bold where it comes in contact with people on a regular basis, such as at a campground. Often seen in small flocks consisting mainly of family members. Feeds on a wide variety of food, but seeds make up 70 percent of the diet. Will cache seeds and acorns for later consumption. Was named after the Arctic explorer Georg W. Steller, who is said to have first recorded the bird on the coast of Alaska in 1741.

Belted Kingfisher
Megaceryle alcyon

YEAR-ROUND
SUMMER
WINTER

Size: 12–14" (30–36 cm)

Male: Blue with white belly, blue-gray chest band, and black wing tips. Ragged crest moves up and down at will. Large head. Long, thick, black bill. White spot by eyes. Red-brown eyes.

Female: same as male but with rusty flanks and a rusty chest band below the blue-gray band

Juvenile: similar to female

Nest: cavity; female and male excavate in a bank of a river, lake or cliff; 1 brood per year

Eggs: 6–7; white without markings

Incubation: 23–24 days; female and male incubate

Fledging: 23–24 days; female and male feed the young

Migration: complete to non-migrator in Alaska

Food: small fish

Compare: Larger than the Steller's Jay (p. 113), which has a black head and more prominent crest. Canada Jay (p. 315) lacks the breast band of the Belted Kingfisher.

Stan's Notes: Usually found at the bank of a river, lake or large stream. Perches on a branch near water, dives in headfirst to catch a small fish, then returns to the branch to feed. Parents drop dead fish into the water to teach their young to dive. Can't pass bones through its digestive tract; regurgitates bone pellets after meals. Gives a loud call that sounds like a machine gun. Mates know each other by their calls. Digs a tunnel up to 4 feet (1 m) long to a nest chamber. Small white patches on dark wing tips flash during flight.

YEAR-ROUND

Chestnut-backed Chickadee
Poecile rufescens

Size: 4¾" (12 cm)

Male: Rich, warm chestnut back and sides. Black crown and chin. White cheeks and sides of head. Gray wings and tail.

Female: same as male

Juvenile: same as adult

Nest: cavity; female and male build; 1–2 broods per year

Eggs: 5–7; white without markings

Incubation: 10–12 days; female incubates

Fledging: 13–16 days; female and male feed the young

Migration: non-migrator

Food: insects, seeds, fruit; comes to seed and suet feeders

Compare: Black-capped Chickadee (p. 267) and Boreal Chickadee (p. 269) lack Chestnut-backed's distinctive chestnut back.

Stan's Notes: The most colorful of all chickadees. Like the other chickadee species, the Chestnut-backed clings to branches upside down, looking for insects. During breeding, it is quiet and secretive. In winter it joins other birds such as kinglets, woodpeckers and other chickadees. Prefers humid coastal coniferous forests with hemlock and Tamarack. Builds a cavity nest 2–20 feet (up to 6 m) above the ground. Will use the same nest year after year. In late summer, some move to higher elevations and back down just before winter starts. Can be attracted to your yard with nest boxes. Comes to seed and suet feeders.

Hoary Redpoll

male

female

Common Redpoll
Acanthis flammea

YEAR-ROUND
SUMMER
WINTER

Size: 5" (13 cm)

Male: Sparrow-like bird with a bright-red crown and raspberry red on the chest. Black spot on the chin. Heavily streaked back.

Female: similar to male but lacks red on the chest

Juvenile: browner than adults, with dark streaking on the chest; lacks a red crown

Nest: cup; female builds; 1 brood (occasionally 2) per year

Eggs: 4–5; pale green with purple markings

Incubation: 10–11 days; female incubates

Fledging: 11–12 days; female and male feed the young

Migration: irruptive; moves around in groups during winter to find food

Food: seeds, insects; will come to seed feeders

Compare: Smaller than Snow Bunting (p. 47), which lacks a red crown. Same size as Pine Siskin (p. 121), which has yellow wing bars and lacks the red crown. Look for the bright red crown and black spot under the bill.

Stan's Notes: Seen throughout Alaska. Visits feeders in small to large flocks. Flocks of up 100 birds are not uncommon but are not seen at all in some winters. Bathes in open water or snow in winter. Like the Black-capped Chickadee, it can be tamed and fed by hand. Gives a zipping call in long strings that last 30 seconds or more. Also gives a nasal, rising whistle. Hoary Redpoll (see inset) is overall paler than Common Redpoll with less streaking on flanks and a pink wash on breast.

Pine Siskin
Spinus pinus

YEAR-ROUND
SUMMER

Size: 5" (13 cm)

Male: Small brown finch with heavy streaking on the back, breast and belly. Yellow wing bars. Yellow at the base of tail. Thin bill.

Female: similar to male, with less yellow

Juvenile: similar to adult, with a light-yellow tinge over the breast and chin

Nest: cup; female builds; 2 broods

Eggs: 3–4; greenish blue with brown markings

Incubation: 12–13 days; female incubates

Fledging: 14–15 days; female and male feed the young

Migration: partial to non-migrator; moves around in search of food

Food: seeds, insects; will come to seed feeders

Compare: Same size as the Common Redpoll (p. 119), which has a red crown and black spot on the chin. Look for the Pine Siskin's streaked breast and yellow wing bars to help identify.

Stan's Notes: A nesting resident in southeastern parts of Alaska. Usually considered a winter finch. More visible in the non-nesting season, when it gathers in flocks, moves around and visits feeders. Nests are often only a few feet apart. Builds nest toward the end of coniferous branches, where needles are dense, helping to conceal. Will come to thistle feeders. Gives a series of high-pitched, wheezy calls. Also gives a wheezing twitter. Breeds in small groups. Male feeds the female during incubation. Juveniles lose the yellow tint by late summer of their first year.

Song Sparrow
Melospiza melodia

Size: 5–6" (13–15 cm)

Male: Common brown sparrow with heavy dark streaks on the chest coalescing into a central dark spot.

Female: same as male

Juvenile: similar to adults, with a finely streaked chest; lacks a central dark spot

Nest: cup; female builds; 2 broods per year

Eggs: 3–4; blue to green, with red-brown markings

Incubation: 12–14 days; female incubates

Fledging: 9–12 days; female and male feed the young

Migration: non-migrator to partial

Food: insects, seeds; only rarely comes to ground feeders with seeds

Compare: Similar to other brown sparrows. Savannah Sparrow (p. 131) is more widespread and has fine brown streaks on its breast. Look for Song Sparrow's heavily streaked breast.

Stan's Notes: There are many subspecies of this bird, but the dark spot in the center of the chest appears in every variety. A constant songster, repeating its loud, clear song every few minutes. The song varies from region to region but has the same basic structure. Sings from thick shrubs to defend a small territory, beginning with three notes and finishing up with a trill. A ground feeder, it will "double-scratch" with both feet at the same time to expose seeds. When the female builds a new nest for a second brood, the male often takes over feeding the first brood. Unlike many other sparrow species, Song Sparrows rarely flock together. A common host of the Brown-headed Cowbird.

Bank Swallow
Riparia riparia

Size: 5¼" (13 cm)

Male: A dull brown-to-gray swallow with a white chin and belly contrasting against a brown breast band. Long pointed wings. Tiny dark bill. Small legs and feet.

Female: same as male

Juvenile: similar to adult, but has a white chin and white extending behind eyes

Nest: cavity; female and male excavate; 1 brood per year

Eggs: 3–7; white without markings

Incubation: 14–16 days; female and male incubate

Fledging: 18–24 days; female and male feed young

Migration: complete to South America

Food: insects

Compare: The Tree Swallow (p. 107) is iridescent blue green and lacks a breast band. Cliff Swallow (p. 127) has a tan-to-rust rump, cheeks and forehead. Barn Swallow (p. 109) has a blue black back and cinnamon belly.

Stan's Notes: A colony swallow that excavates its nest cavity in a riverbank. Nest cavities are often 2–3 feet (up to 1 m) deep and have a feather lining in the nest chamber. Known to use an old Kingfisher nest cavity. Mated pairs will pass a feather back and forth while in flight to strengthen the bond between them. Entire colony tends to breed at the same time (synchronously). Members of the colony lead others to food sources. After young fledge, the colony gathers in extremely large flocks for roosting just before migrating.

SUMMER

Cliff Swallow
Petrochelidon pyrrhonota

Size: 5½" (14 cm)

Male: Uniquely patterned swallow with a dark back, wings and cap. Distinctive tan-to-rust rump, cheeks and forehead.

Female: same as male

Juvenile: similar to adult, lacks distinct patterning

Nest: gourd-shaped, made of mud; male and female build; 1–2 broods per year

Eggs: 4–6; pale white with brown markings

Incubation: 14–16 days; male and female incubate

Fledging: 21–24 days; female and male feed young

Migration: complete, to South America

Food: insects

Compare: Smaller than Barn Swallow (p. 109), which has a distinctive, deeply forked tail and blue back and wings. Bank Swallow (p. 125) is a similar size and lacks the unique tan-to-rust coloring on the rump, cheeks and forehead.

Stan's Notes: Summer resident in parts of Alaska. Common around bridges (especially bridges over water) and rural housing (especially in open country near cliffs). Builds a gourd-shaped nest with a funnel-like entrance pointing down. A colony nester, with many nests lined up beneath building eaves or cliff overhangs. Will carry balls of mud up to a mile to construct its nest. Many in the colony return to the same nest site each year. Not unusual to have two broods per season. If the number of nests underneath eaves becomes a problem, wait until the young have left the nests to hose off the mud.

male
p. 271

female

Dark-eyed Junco
Junco hyemalis

Size: 5½" (14 cm)

Female: A plump, dark-eyed bird with a tan-to-brown chest, head and back. White belly. Ivory-to-pink bill. White outer tail feathers appear like a white V in flight.

Male: round bird with gray plumage

Juvenile: similar to female, with streaking on the breast and head

Nest: cup; female and male build; 2 broods per year

Eggs: 3–5; white with reddish-brown markings

Incubation: 12–13 days; female incubates

Fledging: 10–13 days; male and female feed the young

Migration: partial to complete migrator, throughout the U.S.

Food: seeds, insects; visits ground and seed feeders

Compare: Rarely confused with any other bird. The Dark-eyed Junco is not in Alaska during the winter. Look for the ivory-to-pink bill and small flocks feeding beneath seed feeders to help identify the female Dark-eyed Junco.

Stan's Notes: This is one of Alaska's common summer birds. Adheres to a rigid social hierarchy, with dominant birds chasing the less dominant birds. Look for the white outer tail feathers flashing in flight. Often seen in small flocks on the ground, where it uses its feet to simultaneously "double-scratch" to expose seeds and insects. Eats many weed seeds. Nests in a wide variety of wooded habitats in April and May. Several subspecies of Dark-eyed Junco were previously considered to be separate species but have now been combined into one.

SUMMER

Savannah Sparrow
Passerculus sandwichensis

Size: 5½" (14 cm)

Male: Overall brown bird with fine streaks on the breast and a central dark spot. White belly and chin. Distinctive stripe down center of crown. Dark line extending from the back of each eye and from the base of bill to back of head. Yellowish eyebrows. Small bill.

Female: same as male

Juvenile: similar to adult

Nest: cup; female builds; 1–2 broods per year

Eggs: 3–5; pale green to white, brown markings

Incubation: 10–13 days; female incubates

Fledging: 10–14 days; female and male feed young

Migration: complete, to southwestern states, Mexico

Food: seeds, insects

Compare: The Song Sparrow (p. 123) is not as wide spread and has coarse brown streaks on its breast compared with the fine streaks of the Savannah Sparrow. The Golden-crowned Sparrow (p. 147) is larger and has a black and yellow crown.

Stan's Notes: Common sparrow of various habitats. Sometimes in small flocks. Many geographical variations, ranging from very pale brown and gray to dark brown to nearly black. In Alaska, most are medium brown. Often runs across the ground like a mouse. Some males mate with several females (polygamous). May nest in small groups. Lines nest with moss, grass and hair. Nest is usually flush with the ground in a natural or excavated depression.

American Tree Sparrow
Spizelloides arborea

SUMMER MIGRATION

Size: 6" (15 cm)

Male: Brown with a tan chest and rusty crown and eye line. Gray eyebrows. Dark spot in the center of the chest. Dark upper bill; yellow lower bill. 2 white wing bars.

Female: same as male

Juvenile: streaked chest often obscures the central dark spot; lacks a rusty crown

Nest: cup; female builds; 1 brood per year

Eggs: 3–5; greenish white with brown markings

Incubation: 12–13 days; female incubates

Fledging: 8–10 days; female and male feed the young

Migration: complete, throughout the Lower 48 States

Food: insects, seeds; visits seed feeders

Compare: The Song Sparrow (p. 123) has a heavily streaked chest. To identify the American Tree Sparrow, check for the dark spot on the chest and the two-toned bill.

Stan's Notes: Bird feeder visitor in Alaska during summer. Breeds throughout the state. Commonly seen during migration in flocks of 2–200 birds. Found in open fields, woodlands and suburban backyards. Gives a series of high-pitched, sweet-sounding whistles. Nests in Canada and Alaska. The species name *arborea* means "tree," but it doesn't nest in trees; it nests on the ground in a clump of grass. The "Tree" in the name refers to its habitat. "American" refers to its natural range.

male

female

Gray-crowned Rosy-Finch
Leucosticte tephrocotis

YEAR-ROUND
SUMMER
WINTER

Size: 6" (15 cm)

Male: Gray crown with a black forehead, chin and throat. Warm cinnamon-brown body with a wash of rosy red, especially along flanks and rump.

Female: same as male, but has less red

Juvenile: similar to adult of the same sex

Nest: cup; female builds; 1–2 broods per year

Eggs: 3–5; white without markings

Incubation: 12–14 days; female incubates

Fledging: 16–18 days; female and male feed young

Migration: complete to partial migrator in Alaska, moves around to find food

Food: seeds, insects; will visit seed feeders

Compare: Slightly larger than the female Dark-eyed Junco (p. 129), but has a gray crown, rosy red flanks and dark belly Lapland Longspur (p. 141) is slightly larger and has a rusty red nape.

Stan's Notes: Found in high alpine regions, nesting in steep cliff faces. Breeds throughout most of Alaska. Moves into southern coastal parts of the state in winter. Almost always seen in small flocks, foraging on the ground near patches of snow in high elevations. During breeding, both male and female develop an opening in the floor of the mouth (buccal pouch), which is used to carry a large supply of food, such as insects, to young in the nest. Comes to feeders offering sunflower seeds.

Northern Waterthrush
Parkesia noveboracensis

SUMMER

Size: 6" (15 cm)

Male: A large, overall dark brown warbler. Chest, chin and belly are white to pale yellow with heavy dark streaks. Long narrow eyebrows, white to pale yellow, extending from base of bill to back of head.

Female: same as male

Juvenile: similar to adult

Nest: cup; female builds; 1 brood per year

Eggs: 3–6; pale white with brown markings

Incubation: 10–13 days; female incubates

Fledging: 10–11 days; female and male feed young

Migration: complete, to Mexico, Central America and South America

Food: insects, crustaceans, tiny fish, mollusks

Compare: Larger than Arctic Warbler (p. 265), which shares light eyebrows, but lacks the heavy brown streaking of Northern Waterthrush. The Blackpoll Warbler (p. 45) is slightly smaller and lacks light eyebrows.

Stan's Notes: One of the wood warblers. Found along woodland streams and creeks, where it hunts for insects. Spends much of its time walking along stream banks or wading in shallow water, often flipping leaves, looking for insects to eat. Constructs its nest under roots, rock shelves and overhanging banks near the water's edge. Constantly bobs head and pumps tail up and down while walking, hunting or just after landing.

breeding

winter
p. 281

Least Sandpiper
Calidris minutilla

Size: 6" (15 cm)

Male: Breeding plumage has a golden-brown head and back and a white belly. Dull-yellow legs. White eyebrows and a short, down-curved black bill.

Female: same as male

Juvenile: similar to winter adult but buff-brown and lacks the breast band

Nest: ground; male and female construct; 1 brood per year

Eggs: 3–4; olive with dark markings

Incubation: 19–23 days; male and female incubate

Fledging: 25–28 days; male and female feed the young

Migration: complete, to California, Mexico and Central America

Food: aquatic and terrestrial insects, seeds

Compare: The smallest of sandpipers. Often confused with breeding Western Sandpiper (p. 143), look for Least Sandpiper's yellow legs to differentiate it from other tiny sandpipers. The short, thin down-curved bill also helps to identify.

Stan's Notes: Seen in the southern three-quarters of the state in summer and during migration. This is a tiny, tame sandpiper that can be approached without scaring it. It is the smallest of peeps (sandpipers), nesting on the tundra in Alaska. Prefers the grassy flats of saltwater and freshwater ponds. Its yellow legs can be hard to see in water, poor light or when covered with mud. Most other small shorebirds have black legs and feet.

breeding
male

winter
male

female

Lapland Longspur
Calcarius lapponicus

SUMMER
MIGRATION

Size: 6¼" (15.5 cm)

Male: Breeding male (Mar–Sep) is overall brown with a black head, throat and chest. Tan eyebrows. Rusty red nape. White belly. Small, pointed yellow bill with a black tip. Winter male is much duller and lacks the black head, throat and chest.

Female: very similar to winter male

Juvenile: similar to female, but duller

Nest: cup; female builds; 1 brood per year

Eggs: 3–7; pale green with brown markings

Incubation: 12–13 days; female incubates

Fledging: 8–10 days; male and female feed young

Migration: complete, to northwestern states

Food: insects, seeds

Compare: The Gray-crowned Rosy-Finch (p. 135) is slightly smaller and lacks a rusty red nape. Breeding male Snow Bunting (p. 47) has a white head. Look for the black head to help identify the breeding male Lapland.

Stan's Notes: A summer resident and migrator in Alaska, often seen in open areas and along roads. Often seen in flocks with Horned Larks and Snow Buntings. Common name "Longspur" refers to the long rear toe and nail, which are nearly twice the length of the front two toes. Nests in a shallow depression on the ground in Alaska and Northwest Territories of Canada. One of the widest breeding ranges, extending around the world just south of the polar region (circumpolar). One of four longspur species in North America.

winter p. 283

breeding

Western Sandpiper
Calidris mauri

SUMMER
MIGRATION

Size: 6½" (16 cm)

Male: Breeding has a bright rust-brown crown, ear patch and back and a white chin and chest. Black legs. Narrow bill that droops near tip.

Female: same as male

Juvenile: similar to breeding adult; bright buff-brown on the back only

Nest: ground; male and female construct; 1 brood per year

Eggs: 2–4; light brown with dark markings

Incubation: 20–22 days; male and female incubate

Fledging: 19–21 days; male and female feed the young

Migration: complete, to California, Mexico and Central America

Food: aquatic and terrestrial insects

Compare: Breeding Least Sandpiper (p. 139) lacks the bright rust-brown cap, ear patch and back. Western has a longer bill that droops slightly at the tip. Breeding Red Knot (p. 363) lacks the rusty brown back and white belly.

Stan's Notes: Summer resident along the western coast of Alaska, nesting on the tundra in large "loose" colonies. A long-distance migrant, with adults leaving their breeding grounds several weeks before the young. Some obtain breeding plumage before leaving in spring. Feeds on insects at the water's edge, sometimes immersing its head. Young leave the nest (precocial) within a few hours after hatching. Female leaves and the male tends the hatchlings.

juvenile

SUMMER
WINTER

White-crowned Sparrow
Zonotrichia leucophrys

Size: 6½–7½" (16.5–19 cm)

Male: Brown with a gray chest and black-and-white striped crown. Small, thin, pink bill.

Female: same as male

Juvenile: similar to adults, with black and brown stripes on the head

Nest: cup; female builds; 2 broods per year

Eggs: 3–5; greenish to bluish to whitish with red-brown markings

Incubation: 11–14 days; female incubates

Fledging: 8–12 days; male and female feed the young

Migration: complete, to western coastal states, Mexico

Food: insects, seeds, berries; visits ground feeders

Compare: Golden-crowned Sparrow (p. 147) has a central yellow spot on the crown. The Song Sparrow (p. 123) has heavy dark streaks on the breast coalescing into a central spot. Look for the striped crown to help identify the White-crowned Sparrow.

Stan's Notes: Often in groups of up to 20 birds during migration and summer, when it can be seen visiting ground feeders and feeding beneath seed feeders. This ground feeder will "double-scratch" backward with both feet simultaneously to find seeds. Prefers scrubby areas, woodland edges, and open or grassy habitats. The males are prolific songsters, singing in late winter while migrating north. Males take most of the responsibility for raising the young while females start their second broods. Only 9–12 days separate the broods. Nests in the southern two-thirds of Alaska.

juvenile

winter

SUMMER
WINTER

Golden-crowned Sparrow
Zonotrichia atricapilla

Size: 7" (18 cm)

Male: All-brown sparrow with a heavy body, long tail and yellow spot in the center of a black crown. Gray around head and chest. Upper bill (mandible) is darker than the lower bill (mandible). Winter has varying amounts of black on crown.

Female: same as male

Juvenile: similar to adult, lacks the black and yellow crown

Nest: cup; female and male build; 1 brood a year

Eggs: 3–5; bluish white with brown markings

Incubation: 10–14 days; female incubates

Fledging: 8–14 days; male and female feed the young

Migration: complete, to western coastal U.S., Mexico

Food: insects, seeds, berries

Compare: The White-crowned Sparrow (p. 145) is similar, but it lacks the yellow patch in the center of Golden-crowned's black crown. The Savannah Sparrow (p. 131) is smaller and lacks the black and yellow crown.

Stan's Notes: A common summer bird, breeding in the southern half of Alaska. Often seen in flocks with other sparrows. In the winter there are varying amounts of black on the head, but the yellow patch remains the same. Male feeds the female while she incubates. Nests in western Canada and Alaska. Found in weedy or shrubby areas, along forest edges. A ground feeder often seen scratching the ground under seed and suet feeders. Also feeds on dried and fresh fruits, flower buds and insects.

red morph

Pacific
sooty

SUMMER

Fox Sparrow
Passerella iliaca

Size: 7" (18 cm)

Male: A plump rusty sparrow. Two morphs occur in Alaska. Red morph is rusty red with a heavily streaked rusty breast and solid rust tail. Head and back are mottled with gray Pacific variety is rusty brown with a heavily streaked rusty breast and solid rust tail.

Female: same as male

Juvenile: same as adult

Nest: cup; female builds; 2 broods per year

Eggs: 2–4; pale green with reddish markings

Incubation: 12–14 days; female incubates

Fledging: 10–11 days; male and female feed the young

Migration: complete, to southwestern states, western coastal states

Food: seeds, insects; comes to ground feeders

Compare: Rusty color differentiates the Fox Sparrow from all other sparrows. Look for a heavily streaked chest and long tail to help identify.

Stan's Notes: One of the largest sparrows. Several color variations, depending on the part of the country. Often seen only underneath seed feeders during summer and migration, searching for seeds and insects. Scratches like a chicken with both feet at the same time to find food. Usually solitary or in small groups. The common name "Sparrow" comes from the Anglo-Saxon word *spearwa*, meaning "flutterer," as applied to any small bird. "Fox" refers to the birds rusty color. Nests on the ground in brush and at forest edges in the southern three-quarters of Alaska. Map reflects the combined range.

winter

breeding

Semipalmated Plover
Charadrius semipalmatus

SUMMER

Size: 7" (18 cm)

Male: A brown-backed bird with a white breast and belly. Black crown, mask and necklace. White patch on forehead. Orange eye-ring. Yellow legs. Short, black-tipped orange bill. Winter plumage has a brown mask and lacks the orange eye-ring.

Female: same as male

Juvenile: similar to adult but lacks a well-defined black necklace

Nest: ground; male builds; 1 brood per year

Eggs: 3–4; light brown with dark markings

Incubation: 23–25 days; male and female incubate

Fledging: 22–28 days; male and female feed the young

Migration: complete, to western coastal U.S., Mexico

Food: insects, seeds, worms

Compare: Killdeer (p. 175) shares the brown back and white belly, but it is larger and has 2 black neck bands. Look for a very short bill and single black necklace to help identify the Semipalmated Plover.

Stan's Notes: A breeding bird throughout Alaska. Breeding birds often have orange eye-rings. Hunts by running quickly, stopping to look, then stabbing its prey. Prefers to nest in open rocky places, where the male scrapes out a shallow depression. Nests on the ground on the tundra of northern Canada and Alaska. Populations decreased greatly during the late 1800s due to hunting.

female

male

SUMMER

Horned Lark
Eremophila alpestris

Size: 7–8" (18–20 cm)

Male: Tan to brown with black markings on the face. Black necklace and bill. Pale-yellow chin. Two tiny feather "horns" on the top of the head, sometimes hard to see. Dark tail with white outer tail feathers, seen in flight.

Female: duller than male; less noticeable "horns"

Juvenile: lacks a yellow chin and black markings; does not develop "horns" until the second year

Nest: ground; female builds; 2–3 broods per year

Eggs: 3–4; gray with brown markings

Incubation: 11–12 days; female incubates

Fledging: 9–12 days; female and male feed the young

Migration: complete, to western states and Mexico

Food: seeds, insects

Compare: Slightly larger than most sparrows, with a narrow, sleeker body. Look for the black markings in front of eyes to help identify the Horned Lark.

Stan's Notes: The only true lark native to North America. A bird of open ground. Common in rural areas; often seen in large flocks. The population increased in North America over the past century as more land was cleared for farming. Male performs a fluttering courtship flight high in the air while singing a high-pitched song. Female performs a fluttering distraction display when the nest is disturbed. Can renest about a week after the brood fledges. "Lark" comes from the Middle English *laverock*, or "a lark."

Northern Saw-whet Owl

Aegolius acadicus

Size: 8" (20 cm); up to 17" wingspan

Male: Small tawny brown owl with wide vertical rusty brown streaks on a white breast and belly. Distinctive light marks on back and wings. Short tail. A white face, yellow eyes and small dark bill.

Female: same as male

Juvenile: dark brown with a light brown belly

Nest: cavity, former woodpecker cavity; does not add any nesting material; 1 brood per year

Eggs: 5–6; white without markings

Incubation: 26–28 days; female and male incubate

Fledging: 27–34 days; male and female feed young

Migration: non-migrator in Alaska

Food: mice, small birds, insects

Compare: Great Horned Owl (p. 249) is much larger and has large, obvious ear tufts. The Short-eared Owl (p. 195) is nearly twice as large. Northern Hawk Owl (p. 197) is twice as large and has a long tail.

Stan's Notes: Year-round resident in southeastern coastal Alaska. Our smallest owl, but not often recognized as an owl because of its diminutive size. Usually in coniferous-deciduous forests. Strictly a nighttime hunter. Frequently roosts in cavities in conifers or thick vegetation. Has relatively long wings for such a small raptor. The common name comes from its rarely heard call, a repeated low raspy whistle that is reminiscent of a saw blade being sharpened. Can be very tame and approachable.

winter

breeding

SUMMER

Spotted Sandpiper
Actitis macularius

Size: 8" (20 cm)

Male: Olive-brown back with black spots on a white chest and belly. White line over eyes. Long, dull-yellow legs. Long bill. Winter plumage lacks spots on the chest and belly.

Female: same as male

Juvenile: similar to winter plumage, with a darker bill

Nest: ground; male builds; 2 broods per year

Eggs: 3–4; brownish with brown markings

Incubation: 20–24 days; male incubates

Fledging: 17–21 days; male feeds the young

Migration: complete, to southwestern states, Mexico, Central and South America

Food: aquatic insects

Compare: Smaller than Lesser Yellowlegs (p. 171). The Killdeer (p. 175) has 2 black neck bands. Look for the black spots on the chest and belly and the bobbing tail to help identify the breeding Spotted Sandpiper.

Stan's Notes: One of the few shorebirds that will dive underwater if pursued. Able to fly straight up out of the water. Holds wings in a cup-like arc in flight, rarely lifting them above a horizontal plane. Walks as if delicately balanced. When standing, constantly bobs its tail. Gives a rapid series of "weet-weet-weet" calls when frightened and flying away. Female mates with multiple males and lays eggs in up to five nests. Male does all of the nest building, incubating and childcare without any help from the female. In winter plumage, it lacks the black spots on chest and belly.

winter
p. 291

breeding

Dunlin
Calidris alpina

SUMMER MIGRATION

Size: 8–9" (20–23 cm)

Male: Breeding adult is distinctive with a rusty-red back, finely streaked chest and an obvious black patch on the belly. Stout bill, curving slightly downward at the tip. Black legs.

Female: slightly larger than male, with a longer bill

Juvenile: slightly rusty back with a spotty chest

Nest: ground; male and female construct; 1 brood per year

Eggs: 2–4; olive-buff or blue-green with red-brown markings

Incubation: 21–22 days; male incubates during the day, female incubates at night

Fledging: 19–21 days; male feeds the young, female often leaves before the young fledge

Migration: complete, to western coastal U.S., Mexico and Central America

Food: insects

Compare: Surfbird (p. 303) and breeding Red Knot (p. 363) are larger and lack the large black patch on belly. Look for the Dunlin's stout down-curved bill.

Stan's Notes: Breeding plumage more commonly seen in spring. Flights include heights of up to 100 feet (30 m) with brief gliding alternating with shallow flutters, and a rhythmic, repeating song. Huge flocks fly synchronously, with birds twisting and turning, flashing light and dark undersides. Males tend to fly farther south in winter than females.

Bohemian Waxwing
Bombycilla garrulus

YEAR-ROUND
SUMMER

Size: 8¼" (21 cm)

Male: Very sleek-looking bird, gray to light brown with a gray belly. Pointed crest, bandit-like black mask and black chin. Obvious yellow pattern on black wings. Wing tips look as if they were dipped in red wax. Bright yellow tip of tail and rust undertail.

Female: same as male

Juvenile: gray with a heavily streaked chest, lacks red wing tips

Nest: cup; female constructs; 1 brood per year

Eggs: 4–6; pale blue with dark markings

Incubation: 13–16 days; female incubates

Fledging: 13–16 days; female and male feed the young

Migration: complete to non-migrator, to the southern coast of Alaska and northern states

Food: insects, berries, fruit

Compare: Unique-looking bird, not usually confused with other species. Look for a black mask, pointed crest and rust undertail to identify.

Stan's Notes: Feather shafts in adults exude a red waxy substance. The function is unknown, but it may be a signal of sexual maturity. "Bohemian" refers to its vagabond behavior of wandering in large flocks in fall and winter. The Latin species name *garrulus* means "talkative" or "shattering" and refers to its constant vocalizations. Usually very tame and approachable. Descends upon a single tree that has fruit and remains until nearly all fruit has been consumed. Mature birds have greater nesting success than younger birds.

male
p. 27

female

Red-winged Blackbird
Agelaius phoeniceus

SUMMER

Size: 8½" (22 cm)

Female: Heavily streaked brown body. Pointed brown bill and white eyebrows.

Male: jet black with red-and-yellow shoulder patches (epaulets) and a pointed black bill

Juvenile: same as female

Nest: cup; female builds; 2–3 broods per year

Eggs: 3–4; bluish green with brown markings

Incubation: 10–12 days; female incubates

Fledging: 11–14 days; female and male feed the young

Migration: complete, to western states

Food: seeds, insects; visits seed and suet feeders

Compare: The slightly larger female Rusty Blackbird (p. 295) lacks prominent white eyebrows and streaks on breast.

Stan's Notes: Summer resident in southeastern Alaska. Found around marshes, wetlands, lakes and rivers. Flocks with as many as 10,000 birds have been reported. Males arrive before females and sing to defend their territory. The male repeats his call from the top of a cattail while showing off his red-and-yellow shoulder patches. The female chooses a mate and often builds her nest over shallow water in a thick stand of cattails. The male can be aggressive when defending the nest. Feeds mostly on seeds in spring and fall, and insects throughout the summer.

hunting

YEAR-ROUND

Boreal Owl
Aegolius funereus

Size: 9–11" (28 cm); up to a 21" wingspan

Male: Small brown-to-gray non-eared owl with white spots on the back and wings. White spots and streaks on the breast and belly. Large fluffy head and obvious white facial disk outlined in black. Bright yellow eyes. Small dull yellow bill.

Female: same as male, slightly larger

Juvenile: dark gray to nearly black with prominent white eyebrows and chin and several white spots on the wings

Nest: cavity; 1 brood per year

Eggs: 4–6; white without markings

Incubation: 27–28 days; male feeds female while she incubates eggs

Fledging: 28–33 days; male and female feed the young

Migration: non-migrator

Food: voles, other small animals, birds

Compare: The Northern Saw-whet Owl (p. 155) is slightly smaller and lacks the dark outlining around its facial disk.

Stan's Notes: Named "Boreal" for its nesting habitat in coniferous or boreal forests. Usually seen only when it hunts for mice along roads or in yards by bird feeders. Caches food in crevices, tree forks or other small places; sits on frozen prey to thaw it before eating. Silent flier. Often tame, no responding to the presence of people. Irrupts out of normal range during winters with limited food supply. Generally, females and young move in irruption years.

in flight

juvenile

male

female

in-flight
juvenile

American Kestrel
Falco sparverius

SUMMER

Size: 9–11" (23–28 cm); up to 2' wingspan

Male: Rust-brown back and tail. White breast with dark spots. Two vertical black lines on a white face. Blue-gray wings. Wide black band with a white edge on the tip of a rusty tail.

Female: similar to male but slightly larger, with rust-brown wings and dark bands on the tail

Juvenile: same as adult of the same sex

Nest: cavity; does not build a nest; 1 brood per year

Eggs: 4–5; white with brown markings

Incubation: 29–31 days; male and female incubate

Fledging: 30–31 days; female and male feed the young

Migration: complete, to western states

Food: insects, small mammals and birds, reptiles

Compare: The Peregrine Falcon (p. 327) is much larger and has a dark "hood" marking. Look for the two vertical stripes on the face of the Kestrel. No other small bird of prey has a rusty back and tail.

Stan's Notes: An unusual raptor because the sexes look different (dimorphic). Due to its small size, this falcon was once called a Sparrow Hawk. Hovers near roads, then dives for prey. Watch for it to pump its tail after landing on a perch. Perches nearly upright. Eats many grasshoppers. Adapts quickly to a wooden nest box. Can be extremely vocal, giving a loud series of high-pitched calls. Ability to see ultraviolet (UV) light helps it locate mice and other prey by their urine, which glows bright yellow in UV light.

Taiga

in flight

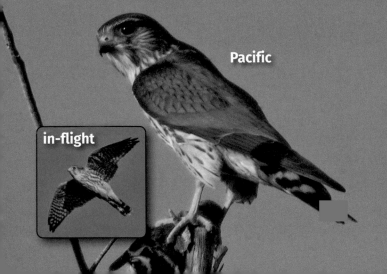

Pacific

in-flight

SUMMER

Merlin
Falco columbarius

Size: 10–12" (25–30 cm); up to 2' wingspan

Male: Streaked brown chest and belly. Light line above each eye. Distinctive wide black tail band and 1–3 very narrow white tail bands. Taiga variety has a steel blue back and darker head and tail. Pacific variety is very dark, with a nearly black back and streaks on the chest.

Female: similar to male but slightly larger, brown head and back, 1–3 narrow buffy tail bands

Juvenile: similar to adult female

Nest: platform or cavity on a cliff; 1 brood per year

Eggs: 4–7; white with rust brown markings

Incubation: 28–32 days; female incubates, male feeds female during incubation

Fledging: 30–35 days; female and male feed the young

Migration: complete, to western states and Central and South America

Food: insects, small mammals and birds, reptiles

Compare: American Kestrel (p. 167) is overall more rusty and has bold vertical mustache marks. The Peregrine Falcon (p. 327) is much larger and has a dark "hood" marking.

Stan's Notes: In urban areas, nests in tall conifers. Appears to move into urban areas in winter. Males hunt and provide food for the female during courtship to show he would be a good provider when she incubates. Formerly called Pigeon Hawk. Also known as Blue-backed Jack due to the blue color of the adult male's back. Catches most of its prey in flight, giving a burst of speed close to the ground rather than diving or hovering like other falcons.

Lesser Yellowlegs
Tringa flavipes

Size:	10–12" (25–30 cm)
Male:	A typical sandpiper-type bird with a brown back and wings. Streaked white chest. Thin, straight black bill. Long yellow legs.
Female:	same as male
Juvenile:	same as adults
Nest:	ground; female builds; 1 brood per year
Eggs:	3–4; yellowish with brown markings
Incubation:	22–23 days; male and female incubate
Fledging:	18–20 days; male and female lead the young to food
Migration:	complete, to South America
Food:	aquatic insects, tiny fish
Compare:	The Greater Yellowlegs (p. 181) is much larger and has a longer, slightly upturned bill. The breeding Spotted Sandpiper (p. 157) has black spots on its chest.

Stan's Notes: Usually seen in small flocks, combing shorelines and mudflats in search of aquatic insects. Usually walks with its head down and tail up, ready to snatch up prey. Uses its long, straight bill to pluck insects and tiny fish out of the water. A member of the sandpiper group known as Tattlers, which scream alarm calls when taking off. Quite often moves into the water before taking flight and gives a variety of flight notes at takeoff. Nest is a simple depression atop a mound of earth. Nests in marshes in the spruce forests of central Alaska and Canada. The nest is a simple depression atop a mound of earth.

winter
p. 307

breeding

SUMMER
MIGRATION

Short-billed Dowitcher
Limnodromus griseus

Size: 11" (28 cm)

Male: Breeding plumage is an overall rusty brown with heavy black spots throughout. Has a small amount of white very low on belly. A long, straight black bill. Off-white eyebrow stripe. Dull yellow-to-green legs and feet.

Female: same as male

Juvenile: similar to winter adult

Nest: ground; female and male construct; 1 brood per year

Eggs: 3–4; olive-green with dark markings

Incubation: 20–21 days; male and female incubate

Fledging: 25–27 days; male and female feed the young

Migration: complete, to coastal Mexico

Food: insects, snails, worms, leeches, seeds

Compare: Same size as breeding Red Knot (p. 363), which has a shorter bill and rich salmon colored head, chest and belly. The breeding Dunlin (p. 159) is smaller and has a black patch on belly.

Stan's Notes: Summer resident seen along southern coastal Alaska and inland on freshwater lakes and marshes. With a rapid probing action like a sewing machine, it uses its long straight bill to probe deep into sand and mud for insects.

SUMMER

Killdeer
Charadrius vociferus

Size: 11" (28 cm)

Male: Upland shorebird with 2 black bands around the neck, like a necklace. Brown back and white belly. Bright reddish-orange rump, visible in flight.

Female: same as male

Juvenile: similar to adults, with a single neck band

Nest: ground; male scrapes; 2 broods per year

Eggs: 3–5; tan with brown markings

Incubation: 24–28 days; male and female incubate

Fledging: 25 days; male and female lead their young to food

Migration: complete, to western states and Mexico

Food: insects, worms, snails

Compare: The Spotted Sandpiper (p. 157) is found around water and lacks the 2 neck bands of the Killdeer. Semipalmated Plover (p. 151) shares the brown back and white belly, but is smaller and has a single black necklace.

Stan's Notes: Technically classified as a shorebird but lives in dry habitats instead of the shore. Often found in vacant fields, gravel pits, driveways, wetland edges or along railroad tracks. The only shorebird that has two black neck bands. Known to fake a broken wing to draw intruders away from the nest; once the nest is safe, the parent will take flight. Nests are just a slight depression in a dry area and are often hard to see. Hatchlings look like miniature adults walking on stilts. Soon after hatching, the young follow their parents around and peck for insects. Gives a loud and distinctive "kill-deer" call. Migrates in small flocks.

male

female

SUMMER

Northern Flicker
Colaptes auratus

Size: 12" (30 cm)

Male: Brown and black with a red mustache and black necklace. Speckled chest. Gray head with a brown cap. Large white rump patch, seen only when flying.

Female: same as male but without a red mustache

Juvenile: same as adult of the same sex

Nest: cavity; female and male excavate; 1 brood per year

Eggs: 5–8; white without markings

Incubation: 11–14 days; female and male incubate

Fledging: 25–28 days; female and male feed the young

Migration: complete, to western states

Food: insects (especially ants and beetles); comes to suet feeders

Compare: The only woodpecker in Alaska that has a brown back. Hairy Woodpecker (p. 53) is smaller and has a white stripe down its back. Look for the speckled breast and gray head of Northern Flicker to help identify.

Stan's Notes: This is the only woodpecker to regularly feed on the ground. Prefers ants and beetles and produces an antacid saliva that neutralizes the acidic defense of ants. Male usually selects a nest site, taking up to 12 days to excavate. Can be attracted to your yard with a nest box stuffed with sawdust. Often reuses an old nest. Undulates deeply during flight, flashing reddish orange under its wings and tail and calling "wacka-wacka" loudly.

SUMMER

Upland Sandpiper
Bartramia longicauda

Size: 12" (30 cm)

Male: Overall brown shorebird. Long yellow legs, a short, brown-tipped yellow bill and white belly. Appears to have a thin neck and small head in relationship to its body.

Female: same as male

Juvenile: similar to adult

Nest: ground; female and male construct; 1 brood per year

Eggs: 3–4; off-white with red markings

Incubation: 21–27 days; female and male incubate

Fledging: 30–31 days; female and male feed young

Migration: complete, to South America

Food: insects, seeds

Compare: Breeding Spotted Sandpiper (p. 157) is smaller, has shorter legs, black spots on a white breast and is found in very different habitats. The Spotted Sandpiper is almost always near water while the Upland is in grassy meadows and prairies.

Stan's Notes: A shorebird of the dry grassland that is aptly named. Often seen standing on fence posts or other perches in a prairie or grassland habitat. Frequently found in prairies and grasslands that were burned, where foraging for food is easier. A true indicator of high-quality prairie habitat, this shorebird returns to a more watery habitat after breeding and just before migrating. Frequently holds its wings open over its back for several seconds just after landing. Formerly known as Upland Plover. Was hunted in the late 1800s.

SUMMER

Greater Yellowlegs
Tringa melanoleuca

Size: 13–15" (33–38 cm)

Male: Tall with a bulbous head and a long, thin, slightly upturned bill. Gray streaking on the chest. White belly. Long yellow legs.

Female: same as male

Juvenile: same as adults

Nest: ground; female builds; 1 brood per year

Eggs: 3–4; off-white with brown markings

Incubation: 22–23 days; female and male incubate

Fledging: 18–20 days; male and female feed the young

Migration: complete, to California, Texas, Mexico and Central and South America

Food: small fish, aquatic insects

Compare: Nearly identical to the Lesser Yellowlegs (p. 171), only larger and has an upturned, longer bill. Whimbrel (p. 213) is larger and lacks the yellow legs.

Stan's Notes: A common shorebird seen in southern parts of Alaska. Can be identified by the slightly upturned bill and long yellow legs, which enable it to wade in deep water. Often seen resting on one leg. Rushes forward through the water to feed, plowing its bill or swinging it from side to side, catching small fish and insects. A skittish bird, it is quick to give an alarm call, causing flocks to take flight. Typically moves into the water before taking flight. Gives a variety of "flight" notes at takeoff. Migrates earlier than Lesser Yellowlegs in spring and later in fall.

breeding
male

winter
p. 373

breeding
female

White-tailed Ptarmigan
Lagopus leucura

YEAR-ROUND

Size: 12½" (32 cm)

Male: Breeding (Apr–Jul) has speckled brown and black sides and a white belly. Red eyebrows (combs). Feathered legs and feet. Small dark bill. White-sided tail, seen in flight.

Female: dark brown with scattered white on sides, feathered legs and feet, small dark bill

Juvenile: similar to breeding female, white on wings

Nest: ground; female builds; 1 brood per year

Eggs: 4–8; tan with brown markings

Incubation: 22–24 days; female incubates

Fledging: 10–15 days; female shows young what to eat

Migration: non-migrator to partial; will move around in winter to find food

Food: leaf and flower buds, seeds, insects, berries

Compare: The breeding Rock Ptarmigan (p. 185) is overall darker. Breeding Willow Ptarmigan (p. 187) is rusty brown. Look for the white sides of tail to help identify.

Stan's Notes: Male displays swollen red combs when courting and alternates fast with slow strutting. Female builds a shallow nest in spring, usually under a shrub, and lines it with fine grass, lichens and feathers. She delays nesting until fully molted into her summer camouflage plumage. If threatened at the nest, female will perform a distraction display that includes hissing and clucking. Male leaves female shortly after eggs hatch. Species name *leucura* is Greek and means "white tail." Other ptarmigans have black-sided tails. Molts in late fall to white plumage and blends into the winter landscape.

breeding
male

winter male
p. 375

breeding
female

Rock Ptarmigan
Lagopus muta

YEAR-ROUND

Size: 14" (36 cm)

Male: Breeding (Apr–Jul) is overall brown, but can be gray to nearly black. Bright red eyebrows (combs). White belly and sides. Small dark bill. Feathered legs and feet. Black-sided tail, seen in flight.

Female: dark brown overall with white wing tips, feathered legs and feet, small dark bill

Juvenile: similar to breeding female, white outermost flight feathers

Nest: ground; female builds; 1 brood per year

Eggs: 6–9; tan with brown markings

Incubation: 21–24 days; female incubates

Fledging: 12–20 days; female shows young what to eat

Migration: non-migrator to partial; will move around in winter to find food

Food: leaf and flower buds, seeds, insects, berries

Compare: The breeding male White-tailed Ptarmigan (p. 183) has black speckles on its sides. The breeding Willow Ptarmigan (p. 187) is rusty brown. Look for black sides on the tail to identify the Rock Ptarmigan.

Stan's Notes: Male displays his bright red combs to female. Female builds a shallow ground nest, usually among rocks, and covers it with vegetation until her clutch is complete. Male leaves the female when she starts to incubate. The common name comes from its habitat on rocky tundra. Latin species name *muta* means "animal that can only mutter or has a weak call" and refers to its quiet call.

breeding male

winter p. 377

breeding female

YEAR-ROUND

Willow Ptarmigan
Lagopus Lagopus

Size: 14" (36 cm)

Male: Breeding plumage (May–Jul) has a rusty red head, neck and upper breast. Brown back and top of wings. White lower breast and belly; often speckled with rusty red. Dark red eyebrows. Feathered legs and feet. Stout dark bill. Black edges on tail, seen in flight.

Female: light brown overall, feathered legs and feet, stout dark bill

Juvenile: similar to breeding female, white on wings

Nest: ground; female builds; 1 brood per year

Eggs: 5–14; blackish brown with cream markings

Incubation: 21–23 days; female incubates

Fledging: 10–14 days; female shows young what to eat

Migration: non-migrator to partial; will move around in winter to find food

Food: buds (mainly willow), seeds, insects

Compare: Breeding Rock Ptarmigan (p. 185) and White-tailed Ptarmigan (p. 183) lack the rusty red head, neck and upper breast.

Stan's Notes: "Ptarmigan" comes from a Gaelic word for this kind of bird, *tarmachan*. Common name comes from its favor for willow buds and leaves. In spring, female molts to a camouflage coloration that enables her to blend with landscape during incubation. Nests on open tundra. Lines its nest with leaves, grass and a few feathers. Unlike other ptarmigan species, male remains with female to raise young. However, the females without mates are just as successful, rearing their young as the females with mates.

male
p. 67

female

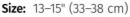

Bufflehead
Bucephala albeola

SUMMER
MIGRATION
WINTER

Size: 13–15" (33–38 cm)

Female: Brownish-gray duck with a dark brown head. White patch on cheek, just behind the eyes.

Male: striking black-and-white duck with a large bonnet-like white patch on the back of head; head shines greenish-purple in sunlight

Juvenile: similar to female

Nest: cavity; female lines an old woodpecker cavity; 1 brood per year

Eggs: 8–10; ivory-to-olive without markings

Incubation: 29–31 days; female incubates

Fledging: 50–55 days; female leads the young to food

Migration: complete, to southern coastal Alaska, western states, Mexico and Central America

Food: aquatic insects, crustaceans, mollusks

Compare: The female Lesser Scaup (p. 199) is slightly larger and has a white patch at the base of the bill. Look for the white cheek patch to help identify the female Bufflehead.

Stan's Notes: Common diving duck that travels with other ducks. Found on rivers and lakes. Nests in vacant woodpecker holes. When cavities in trees are scarce, known to use a burrow in an earthen bank or will use a nest box. Lines the cavity with fluffy down feathers. Unlike other ducks, the young stay in the nest for up to two days before they venture out with their mothers. Female is very territorial and remains with the same mate for many years.

male

female

Green-winged Teal
Anas crecca

YEAR-ROUND
SUMMER

Size: 14–15" (36–38 cm)

Male: Chestnut head with a dark-green patch outlined with white from the eyes to the nape of neck. Gray body and butter-yellow tail. Green patch on the wings (speculum), seen in flight.

Female: light-brown duck with black spots and a green speculum, small bill

Juvenile: same as female

Nest: ground; female builds; 1 brood per year

Eggs: 8–10; cream-white without markings

Incubation: 21–23 days; female incubates

Fledging: 32–34 days; female teaches the young to feed

Migration: complete to non-migrator in Alaska

Food: aquatic plants and insects

Compare: The female Blue-winged Teal (p. 193) is similar in size, but has slight white at base of bill. Look for a dark green patch on each side of a chestnut head to identify the male Green-winged Teal.

Stan's Notes: One of the smallest dabbling ducks. Tips forward in water to feed off the bottom of shallow ponds. This behavior makes it vulnerable to ingesting spent lead shot, which can cause death. It walks well on land and will also feed in flooded fields and woodlands. Known for its fast and agile flight, groups spin and wheel through the air in tight formation. The green wing patches are most obvious during flight.

male

female

Blue-winged Teal
Spatula discors

Size: 15–16" (38–41 cm)

Male: Small, plain-looking brown duck with black speckles and a large, crescent-shaped white mark at the base of the bill. Gray head. Black tail with a small white patch. Blue wing patch (speculum), best seen in flight.

Female: duller than male, with only slight white at the base of the bill; lacks a crescent mark on the face and a white patch on the tail

Juvenile: same as female

Nest: ground; female builds; 1 brood per year

Eggs: 8–11; creamy white

Incubation: 23–27 days; female incubates

Fledging: 35–44 days; female feeds the young

Migration: complete, to western states and Mexico

Food: aquatic plants, seeds, aquatic insects

Compare: The female Mallard (p. 231) has an orange-and-black bill. Female Green-winged Teal (p. 191) is similar in size but lacks white at base of bill. Look for the white facial mark to identify the male Blue-winged.

Stan's Notes: One of the smallest ducks in North America. Constructs nest some distance from water. Female performs a distraction display to protect nest and young. Male leaves female near the end of incubation. Planting crops and cultivating to pond edges have caused a decline in population. Widespread nesting in North America, breeding as far north as central Alaska. One of the most common and longest distance migrating ducks.

hunting

Short-eared Owl
Asio flammeus

Size: 15½" (39 cm); up to 3' wingspan

Male: Overall brown to gray with a large round head and light face. Heavy streaking on the chest with lighter belly Spotted back. Black "wrist" mark. Very short, tiny ear tufts, often not noticeable. Bright yellow eyes and dark eye patches.

Female: same as male, but overall darker

Juvenile: similar to adults, light gray with a dark face

Nest: ground; depression scraped just deep enough to stop eggs from rolling away; 1 brood per year

Eggs: 4–6; white without markings

Incubation: 26–28 days; female incubates

Fledging: 23–26 days; male and female feed young

Migration: complete migrator

Food: small mammals, birds

Compare: Northern Hawk Owl (p. 197) is similar in size, but it has a much smaller head and longer tail. Stiff wing beats and erratic flight make the Short-eared Owl easy to identify.

Stan's Notes: Seen throughout Alaska in summer and year-round along the southeastern coast. Hunts over open fields, often floating on its long wings just before dropping onto prey. Flies with long, slow wing beats. Male calls from high above the nest site, soaring, occasionally swooping and clapping wings together beneath its body. Perches on the ground. Distinctive black "wrist" mark under wings and a bold tan patch near upper end of wings, seen in flight.

swooping

Northern Hawk Owl
Surnia ulula

YEAR-ROUND

Size: 16" (40 cm); up to 2½' wingspan

Male: Overall brown to gray. Many fine rusty bars horizontally from breast to tail. White face with a black frame. Dark and light speckled forehead. Broad, flat top of head and bright yellow eyes. Long pointed tail. Yellow bill.

Female: same as male, only slightly larger

Juvenile: light gray with a dark face, yellow eyes

Nest: cavity or platform; takes over crow or hawk nest, sometimes on top of stump, does not add any nesting material; 1 brood per year

Eggs: 5–7; white without markings

Incubation: 25–30 days; female incubates

Fledging: 25–35 days; male and female feed young

Migration: non-migrator to irruptive; moves around Alaska in winter to find food

Food: mice, other small mammals, birds, insects

Compare: Similar size as Short-eared Owl (p. 195), but has a smaller head and longer tail. Look for Hawk Owls powerful hawk-like flight and swooping approach before landing.

Stan's Notes: A uniquely shaped owl that flies like a hawk (hence its common name) with fast, stiff wing beats. Flies close to ground, swooping up to a perch on a pole or tree. Can hover. Often covers feet while perching. Frequently hunts during the day. Caches extra mice and voles in the forks of trees. Will use a nest box on a tree. Usually unafraid of people.

female

male p. 73

Lesser Scaup
Aythya affinis

SUMMER
MIGRATION

Size: 16–17" (40–43 cm)

Female: Overall brown duck with a dull-white patch at the base of a light-gray bill. Yellow eyes.

Male: white and gray; the chest and head appear nearly black but the head looks purple with green highlights in direct sun; yellow eyes

Juvenile: same as female

Nest: ground; female builds; 1 brood per year

Eggs: 8–14; olive-buff without markings

Incubation: 22–28 days; female incubates

Fledging: 45–50 days; female teaches young to feed

Migration: complete, to western states and Mexico

Food: aquatic plants and insects

Compare: Nearly identical to the female Greater Scaup (p. 217), which has a more rounded head and a bold white patch at the base of bill. The male Blue-winged Teal (p. 193) has a large crescent-shaped white mark at base of bill. The female Canvasback (p. 239) has a sloping forehead and long dark bill.

Stan's Notes: A common diving duck. Often seen in large flocks on lakes, ponds and sewage lagoons. Submerges itself completely to feed on the bottom of lakes (unlike dabbling ducks, which only tip forward to reach the bottom). Note the bold white stripe under the wings when in flight. The male leaves the female when she starts incubating eggs. The quantity of eggs (clutch size) increases with the female's age. This species has an interesting babysitting arrangement in which groups of young (creches) are tended by one to three adult females.

male p. 75

female

Ring-necked Duck
Aythya collaris

SUMMER

Size: 16–19" (41–48 cm)

Female: Brown with a darker-brown back and crown and lighter-brown sides. Gray face. White eye-ring with a white line behind the eye. White ring around the bill. Peaked head.

Male: black head, chest and back; gray-to-white sides; blue bill with a bold white ring and a thinner ring at the base; peaked head

Juvenile: similar to female

Nest: ground; female builds; 1 brood per year

Eggs: 8–10; olive to brown without markings

Incubation: 26–27 days; female incubates

Fledging: 49–56 days; female teaches the young to feed

Migration: complete, to southern states and Mexico

Food: aquatic plants and insects

Compare: Female Lesser Scaup (p. 199) is similar in size. Look for the white ring around the bill to help identify the female Ring-necked Duck.

Stan's Notes: Often seen in larger freshwater lakes, usually in small flocks or just pairs. A diving duck, watch for it to dive underwater to forage for food. Springs up off the water to take flight. Has a distinctive tall, peaked head with a sloped forehead. Flattens its crown when diving. Male gives a quick series of grating barks and grunts. Female gives high-pitched peeps. Named "Ring-necked" for its cinnamon collar, which is nearly impossible to see in the field. Also called Ring-billed Duck due to the white ring on its bill.

male
p. 77

female

SUMMER
MIGRATION

Harlequin Duck
Histrionicus histrionicus

Size: 17" (43 cm)

Male: Overall brown duck with a white patch on the sides of head and near the base of bill. Short bill. Long pointed tail.

Female: black and white duck with rusty red sides and top of head, highest part of head above eyes, small light-colored bill, long pointed tail; winter is overall brown with a white patch at base of bill and sides of head, faint white marks at shoulders and base of tail

Juvenile: similar to female

Nest: ground; female builds; 1 brood per year

Eggs: 6–8; pale white without markings

Incubation: 28–31 days; female incubates

Fledging: 60–70 days; female leads young to food

Migration: complete migrator, to western states

Food: aquatic insects, crustaceans, mollusks

Compare: Same size as the female Long-tailed Duck (p. 79), which has white around the eyes and a large white rump.

Stan's Notes: A small duck that rides low in water. Found in fast running rivers and streams, which presumably have a richer food supply than slow-moving water. Frequently walks in shallow water, foraging for food on the bottom among the rocks. Uses wings and feet to propel itself underwater unlike other diving ducks, which just use their feet. Female does not breed until 2 years of age. Male leaves female after she starts to incubate.

YEAR-ROUND

Sharp-tailed Grouse
Tympanuchus phasianellus

Size: 16–18" (40–45 cm); up to 2' wingspan

Male: Overall brown with white and dark brown-to-black markings. Paler below. Small crest. Yellow eyebrows (combs). Pale purple throat sacs. A narrow, pointed white tail.

Female: similar to non-displaying male

Juvenile: similar to female

Nest: ground; female builds; 1 brood per year

Eggs: 5–15; light brown with brown markings

Incubation: 21–24 days; female incubates

Fledging: 7–10 days; female leads the young to food

Migration: non-migrator; moves around to find food

Food: seeds, nuts, insects, berries, leaves

Compare: Ruffed Grouse (p. 207) is similar in size, but it has a squared dark tail. Male Spruce Grouse (p. 209) has red eyebrows and is dark brown to nearly black. Look for the Sharp-tailed's narrow, pointed white tail.

Stan's Notes: An upland game species named for its pointed tail. Males gather in groups of up to 20 birds in an area called a lek to dance and display. Leks are often used for many years. Displaying males bow forward, droop their wings at their sides and point their tails straight up in the air. Appearing like a wind-up toy, they stamp their feet quickly and produce a loud rattling noise that resonates from the throat sac, which is inflated with air. Females choose the best dancers, which tend to be the older, more experienced males. Often these males are in the center of the group.

drumming

Ruffed Grouse
Bonasa umbellus

YEAR-ROUND

Size: 16–19" (41–48 cm); up to 2' wingspan

Male: Brown chicken-like bird with a long, squared tail. Wide black band near tip of tail. Tuft of feathers on head (crest) appears like a crown when raised. Black ruffs on the sides of neck.

Female: same as male, but has less obvious neck ruffs

Juvenile: same as female

Nest: ground; female builds; 1 brood per year

Eggs: 9–12; tan with light brown markings

Incubation: 23–24 days; female incubates

Fledging: 10–12 days; female leads the young to food

Migration: non-migrator, moves around to find food

Food: seeds, insects, fruit, leaf buds

Compare: Slightly larger and lighter brown than the Spruce Grouse (p. 209), which has a darker tail. Look for feathered tuft on head and black neck ruffs.

Stan's Notes: A common bird of deep woods. Often seen in aspen or other trees, feeding on leaf buds. In the colder northern climates, scaly bristles grow on its feet during winter and serve as snowshoes. When there is enough snow, it dives into a snowbank to roost at night. In spring, the male attracts females by raising its feather tuft, fanning its tail like a turkey and standing on a log, drumming with its wings. The drumming sound is not made by its wings pounding against its chest or hitting the log, but by the air being moved by its cupped wings. Female performs a distraction display to protect her young. Two color morphs, red and gray, most apparent in the tail. Named for the black ruffs on its neck.

Spruce Grouse
Falcipennis canadensis

YEAR-ROUND

Size: 17" (43 cm); up to 2' wingspan

Male: Plump grouse, brown to almost black, with white speckles on the chest and belly Short neck, red eyebrows (combs) and short dark tail with a chestnut tip.

Female: overall brown grouse with small black and white barring on the chest, dark brown tail with a chestnut tip

Juvenile: similar to female

Nest: ground; female builds; 1 brood per year

Eggs: 4–7; tan with brown markings

Incubation: 17–24 days; female incubates

Fledging: 8–10 days; male and female feed young

Migration: non-migrator; moves around to find food

Food: coniferous needles, insects, seeds, berries

Compare: Ruffed Grouse (p. 207) is lighter brown and has a tuft of feathers on the head. The Sharp-tailed Grouse (p. 205) has yellow eyebrows and a narrow, pointed white tail.

Stan's Notes: Well known for being semi-tame and approachable. In winter it is often seen in groups along roads, where snow isn't as deep and small rocks can be eaten to aid in digestion. Prefers open coniferous forests. Eats mainly spruce needles, hence its common name. Roosts in trees. Displaying male fans tail, leans forward and droops wings while quickly flapping wings in a short flight. Female is territorial against other females. The cryptic coloring of the female allows her to blend in with the surroundings. Often freezes when danger approaches, hence its other common name, Fool Hen.

SUMMER
MIGRATION

Bristle-thighed Curlew
Numenius tahitiensis

Size: 17½" (44 cm)

Male: Brown shorebird with a long down-curved bill, dark cap and dark brown line through the eyes. Rusty red wing linings. Pale rump. Gray legs and feet.

Female: same as male

Juvenile: similar to adult

Nest: ground; female and male construct; 1 brood per year

Eggs: 3–5; pale olive green with brown markings

Incubation: 27–30 days; female and male incubate

Fledging: 32–42 days; female and male feed young

Migration: complete, to Pacific islands

Food: insects, fruit, seeds

Compare: Nearly identical to the Whimbrel (p. 213), which has brown-to-gray wing linings and a brown rump.

Stan's Notes: A bird of the mountain tundra. Nests in dry exposed ridges made from lichens, with little or no lining. Seen wintering on Pacific islands but it was unknown where nesting grounds were located until the 1940s, when it was discovered nesting on high mountains in northwestern Alaska. Has a relatively short migration compared with other shorebirds. Unlike the widespread range of the Whimbrel, the Bristle-thighed has a limited range in Alaska.

SUMMER MIGRATION

Whimbrel
Numenius phaeopus

Size: 18" (45 cm)

Male: Heavily streaked bird, light brown to gray. A long down-curved bill and multiple dark brown stripes on the crown. Brown-to-gray wing linings. Dark line through eyes. Legs are light gray to blue.

Female: same as male

Juvenile: similar to adult

Nest: ground; female and male construct; 1 brood per year

Eggs: 3–4; olive green with dark markings

Incubation: 27–28 days; male and female incubate

Fledging: 35–42 days; female and male feed young

Migration: complete, to coastal California and Mexico

Food: insects, snails, worms, leeches, berries

Compare: Bristle-thighed Curlew (p. 211) has rusty red wing linings and rump. The Greater Yellowlegs (p. 181) has yellow legs. Short-billed Dowitcher (p. 173) has a straight bill. The breeding Red Knot (p. 363) has a reddish belly and a much shorter bill.

Stan's Notes: Seen during migration, whimbrels also breed in Alaska. Easy to identify by its very long down-curved bill and brown stripes on head. Uses its bill to probe deep into sand and mud for insects. Unlike the other shorebirds, berries are an important food source in summer. Very vocal, giving single note whistles. Doesn't breed until age 3. Has a long-term pair bond. Adults leave breeding grounds up to two weeks before the young leave.

winter

breeding
p. 87

Red-necked Grebe
Podiceps grisegena

YEAR-ROUND
SUMMER
MIGRATION
WINTER

Size: 18" (45 cm)

Male: Winter (Sep–Mar) is overall brown with a large, slightly darker head and lighter neck. Long, thin yellow bill.

Female: same as male

Juvenile: similar to winter adult

Nest: floating platform; female and male build; 1 brood per year

Eggs: 3–6; white without markings

Incubation: 21–23 days; female and male incubate

Fledging: 50–70 days; female and male feed young

Migration: complete to non-migrator in Alaska

Food: aquatic insects, small fish

Compare: The winter Common Murre (p. 81) and winter Thick-billed Murre (p. 83) have a brownish black back and white lower body.

Stan's Notes: One of seven grebe species in North America. Like the other grebes, it has a tiny tail that is usually hidden in its fluffy feathers at the base of tail (coverts). It has lobed toes unlike ducks, which have webbed feet. Found in small ponds and shallow lakes lined with reeds and sedges. Forages for food by diving for aquatic insects, often remaining underwater for up to a minute. Doesn't fly much once at nesting grounds. Builds a floating nest with plants and anchors it to one spot. Floating keeps nest from submerging when water rises during spring snowmelt. Young hatch one day at a time (asynchronously). Parents feed the young tiny feathers. This presumably helps protect the stomach lining from bones in fish, its main diet. Populations have decreased over the past 30 years.

male
p. 85

female

Greater Scaup
Aythya marila

YEAR-ROUND
SUMMER
MIGRATION
WINTER

Size: 18" (45 cm)

Female: An overall brown duck with a darker head and a bold white patch at the base of bill. Might show a white patch behind each eye. Rounded top of head.

Male: mostly black and white, black head shines green in direct sunlight, bright white sides and a gray back, light blue bill with a black tip, rounded head

Juvenile: same as female

Nest: ground; female builds; 1 brood per year

Eggs: 7–10; greenish olive without markings

Incubation: 24–28 days; female incubates

Fledging: 45–50 days; female teaches young to feed

Migration: complete to non-migrator, to western coastal U.S., Mexico

Food: aquatic plants and insects

Compare: The female Lesser Scaup (p. 199) is very similar, but has a more pointed head and lacks the bold white patch at base of bill. Female Canvasback (p. 239) is larger and has a sloping forehead and long dark bill.

Stan's Notes: Common summer resident and migrant, breeding in the southern two-thirds of Alaska. More common than the Lesser Scaup, but before 1920, the Lesser Scaup was more common. Most abundant on large saltwater bays.

in flight

male

in flight

female

American Wigeon
Anas americana

YEAR-ROUND
SUMMER
MIGRATION

Size: 18–20" (48 cm)

Male: Brown duck with a rounded head and obvious white cap. Deep-green patch starting behind the eyes and streaking down the neck. Long pointed tail. Short, black-tipped grayish bill. White belly and wing linings, seen in flight. Nonbreeding lacks white cap and green patch.

Female: light brown with a pale-gray head, a short, black-tipped grayish bill, green wing patch (speculum) and dark eye spot; white belly and wing linings, seen in flight

Juvenile: similar to female

Nest: ground; female builds; 1 brood per year

Eggs: 7–12; white without markings

Incubation: 23–25 days; female incubates

Fledging: 37–48 days; female teaches the young to feed

Migration: complete to non-migrator, to western states and Mexico

Food: aquatic plants, seeds

Compare: Male American Wigeon is easily identified by the white cap and black-tipped grayish bill. Look for a black-tipped grayish bill and green wing patch to help identify the female American Wigeon.

Stan's Notes: Often in small flocks or with other ducks. Prefers shallow lakes. Male stays with the female only during the first week of incubation. Female raises the young. If threatened, female feigns injury while the young run and hide. Conceals upland nest in tall vegetation within 50–250 yards (46–229 m) of water.

male
p. 89

female

Barrow's Goldeneye
Bucephala islandica

SUMMER
WINTER

Size: 18–20" (45–50 cm)

Female: A large dark brown head. Gray body. Bright golden eyes. Small mostly yellow bill. White collar around neck, often hidden.

Male: black and white duck with large puffy head, head appears deep green in bright sunlight, a low, flat top of head, bright golden eyes, large crescent-shaped white mark in front of each eye, small dark bill

Juvenile: same as female, but has a dark bill

Nest: cavity; female lines old woodpecker cavity; 1 brood per year

Eggs: 9–11; green to olive without markings

Incubation: 32–34 days; female incubates

Fledging: 55–60 days; female leads young to food

Migration: partial migrator, to southern coastal Alaska and western coastal states

Food: aquatic insects and plants, mollusks

Compare: Nearly identical to the female Common Goldeneye (p. 223), which has a yellow tipped dark bill.

Stan's Notes: Nests in cavities near ponds and lakes. Will also use a nest box. Female often returns to the same nest location for many years. Female may mate with the same male from year to year. Male leaves female once she starts incubating. Nestlings leave the nest in just 24–36 hours. Often swims out to open water when threatened instead of flying away. Will hybridize with the closely related Common Goldeneye, producing a bird with a maroon head.

221

female

male
p. 91

Common Goldeneye
Bucephala clangula

SUMMER
WINTER

Size: 18–20" (45–51 cm)

Female: Brown and gray duck with a large dark-brown head and gray body. White collar. Bright-golden eyes. Yellow-tipped dark bill.

Male: mostly white with a black back, a puffy green head, a large white spot on the face, bright-golden eyes and a dark bill

Juvenile: same as female but with a dark bill

Nest: cavity; female lines an old woodpecker cavity; 1 brood per year

Eggs: 8–10; light green without markings

Incubation: 28–32 days; female incubates

Fledging: 56–59 days; female leads the young to food

Migration: complete, to southern coastal Alaska, western states and Mexico

Food: aquatic plants, insects, fish, mollusks

Compare: The female Barrow's Goldeneye (p. 221) is nearly identical, but has a yellow bill. The female Lesser Scaup (p. 199) is similar, but smaller. Look for the female Common Goldeneyes' large dark brown head and white collar.

Stan's Notes: Known for the loud whistling sound produced by its wings during flight. During late winter and early spring, the male performs elaborate mating displays that include throwing his head back and calling a raspy note. Female will lay some of her eggs in other goldeneye nests or in the nests of other species (egg dumping), causing some mothers to incubate as many as 30 eggs in a brood. Named for its bright-golden eyes.

male
p. 325

female

Gadwall
Mareca strepera

Size: 19" (48 cm)

Female: Mottled brown with a pronounced color change from dark-brown body to light-brown neck and head. Bright-white wing linings, seen in flight. Small white wing patch, seen when swimming. Gray bill with orange sides.

Male: plump gray duck with a brown head and distinctive black rump, white belly, bright-white wing linings, small white wing patch, chestnut-tinged wings, gray bill

Juvenile: similar to female

Nest: ground; female lines the nest with fine grass and down feathers plucked from her chest; 1 brood per year

Eggs: 8–11; white without markings

Incubation: 24–27 days; female incubates

Fledging: 48–56 days; young feed themselves

Migration: partial to non-migrator in Alaska

Food: aquatic plants and insects

Compare: Female Mallard (p. 231) is similar but has a blue-and-white wing mark. Look for Gadwall's white wing patch and gray bill with orange sides.

Stan's Notes: A duck of shallow marshes. Consumes mostly plant material, dunking its head in water to feed rather than tipping forward, like other dabbling ducks. Walks well on land; feeds in fields and woodlands. Nests within 300 feet (90 m) of water. Often in pairs with other duck species. Establishes pair bond during winter.

male p. 365

female

SUMMER

Redhead
Aythya americana

Size: 19" (48 cm)

Female: Soft-brown, plain-looking duck with gray-to-white wing linings. Rounded top of head. Two-toned bill, gray with a black tip.

Male: rich-red head and neck with a black chest and tail, gray sides, smoky-gray wings and back, tricolored bill with a light-blue base, white ring and black tip

Juvenile: similar to female

Nest: cup; female builds; 1 brood per year

Eggs: 9–14; pale white without markings

Incubation: 24–28 days; female and male incubate

Fledging: 56–73 days; female shows young what to eat

Migration: complete migrator, to southwestern states, Mexico and Central America

Food: seeds, aquatic plants, insects

Compare: Female Northern Shoveler (p. 229) is similar, but it is lighter brown and has an exceptionally large, shovel-shaped bill.

Stan's Notes: A duck of permanent large bodies of water. Forages along the shoreline, feeding on seeds, aquatic plants and insects. Usually builds nest directly on the water's surface, using large mats of vegetation. Female lays up to 75 percent of its eggs in the nests of other Redheads and several other duck species. Nests primarily in the Prairie Pothole region of the northern Great Plains. Overall populations seem to be increasing at about 2–3 percent each year.

male p. 347

female

Northern Shoveler
Anas clypeata

SUMMER

Size: 19–21" (48–53 cm)

Female: A medium-sized brown duck speckled with black. Green patch on the wings (speculum). An extraordinarily large, spoon-shaped bill.

Male: iridescent green head, rusty sides, white chest and a large spoon-shaped bill

Juvenile: same as female

Nest: ground; female builds; 1 brood per year

Eggs: 9–12; olive without markings

Incubation: 22–25 days; female incubates

Fledging: 30–60 days; female leads the young to food

Migration: complete, to southwestern states, Mexico

Food: aquatic insects, plants

Compare: Female Mallard (p. 231) is similar but lacks the Shoveler's large bill. Look for Shoveler's large spoon-shaped bill to help identify.

Stan's Notes: One of several species of shovelers. Called "Shoveler" due to the peculiar, shovel-like shape of its bill. Given the common name "Northern" because it is the only species of these ducks in North America. Seen in shallow wetlands, ponds and small lakes in flocks of 5–10 birds. Flocks fly in tight formation. Swims low in water, pointing its large bill toward the water as if it's too heavy to lift. Usually swims in tight circles while feeding. Feeds mainly by filtering tiny aquatic insects and plants from the surface of the water with its bill.

male
p. 345

female

Mallard
Anas platyrhynchos

YEAR-ROUND
SUMMER
WINTER

Size:	19–21" (48–53 cm)
Female:	Brown duck with a blue-and-white wing mark (speculum). Orange-and-black bill.
Male:	large green head, white necklace, rust-brown or chestnut chest, combination of gray-and-white sides, yellow bill, orange legs and feet
Juvenile:	same as female but with a yellow bill
Nest:	ground; female builds; 1 brood per year
Eggs:	7–10; greenish to whitish, unmarked
Incubation:	26–30 days; female incubates
Fledging:	42–52 days; female leads the young to food
Migration:	complete to non-migrator in parts of Alaska
Food:	seeds, plants, aquatic insects; will come to ground feeders offering corn
Compare:	Female Northern Pintail (p. 241) is similar to the female Mallard, but has a gray bill. Female Northern Shoveler (p. 229) is the same size, but has a large spoon-shaped bill.

Stan's Notes: A familiar dabbling duck of lakes and ponds. Also found in rivers, streams and some backyards. Tips forward to feed on vegetation on the bottom of shallow water. The name "Mallard" comes from the Latin word *masculus,* meaning "male," referring to the male's habit of taking no part in raising the young. Female and male have white underwings and white tails, but only the male has black central tail feathers that curl upward. The female gives a classic quack. Returns to its birthplace each year.

male
p. 35

female

SUMMER
WINTER

Black Scoter
Melanitta americana

Size: 19¼" (49 cm)

Female: An all-brown duck with a dark crown, pale white cheeks and thin dark bill.

Male: all-black duck with a large yellow knob at the base of bill and a narrow pointed tail

Juvenile: similar to female

Nest: ground; female builds; 1 brood per year

Eggs: 6–8; light pink to buff without markings

Incubation: 30–31 days; female incubates

Fledging: 45–50 days; female feeds young

Migration: partial migrator, to southern coastal Alaska, western coastal U.S. and Mexico

Food: mollusks, crustaceans, aquatic plants, seeds

Compare: Smaller than female White-winged Scoter (p. 237), which has a white patch in front of each eye and a larger bill. Slightly smaller than female Surf Scoter (p. 235), which has a vertical white patch at the base of bill and a white mark on the nape.

Stan's Notes: The least common of scoters, although once known as the Common Scoter. Often in mixed flocks numbering in the hundreds along the coast during migration and winter. Usually will feed in seawater 20-40 feet (6-12 m) deep, just outside the breaker zone. Nests on the tundra close to freshwater lakes and ponds, returning to sea after breeding season for the rest of the summer and winter. Female doesn't breed until her third summer. Male will leave female shortly after she starts to incubate. Broods sometimes gather in groups called creches and are tended by 1-3 older females.

male
p. 93

female

Surf Scoter
Melanitta perspicillata

SUMMER
MIGRATION
WINTER

Size: 20" (50 cm)

Female: Brown duck with a dark crown and white mark on nape. Vertical white patch at the base of a large dark bill.

Male: black with a white patch on forehead and nape, multicolored bill with a white base, black spot and orange tip, bright white eyes

Juvenile: similar to female

Nest: ground; female builds; 1 brood per year

Eggs: 5–8; light pink to buff without markings

Incubation: 30–31 days; female incubates

Fledging: 45–50 days; female feeds young

Migration: partial to complete, to southern coastal Alaska, western coastal U.S. and Mexico

Food: mollusks, crustaceans, aquatic insects

Compare: Slightly larger than the female Black Scoter (p. 233), which has white cheeks and a much smaller bill. Slightly smaller than the female White-winged Scoter (p. 237), which lacks the vertical white patch at the base of its bill and white mark on nape.

Stan's Notes: Dives or scoots through breaking surf. However, the common name "Scoter" may refer to the sooty black color of its plumage. Dives down to 40 feet (12 m) in seawater, foraging for mussels and crustaceans. Fish eggs make up 90 percent of its diet during spring and early summer. Nests on the tundra in Alaska near freshwater lakes and ponds. Spends the winter at sea, rarely returning to shore. Sometimes in mixed flocks with other scoters.

male
p. 37

female

White-winged Scoter
Melanitta fusca

SUMMER
MIGRATION
WINTER

Size: 20½" (52 cm)

Female: Brown duck with a dark crown. Large dull white patch just behind the eyes and at the base of a large dark bill.

Male: black duck with a white patch underneath each eye, large bicolored yellow and orange bill, bright white eyes

Juvenile: similar to female

Nest: ground; female builds; 1 brood per year

Eggs: 5–10; light pink to buff without markings

Incubation: 28–31 days; female incubates

Fledging: 50–60 days; female feeds young

Migration: complete, to southern coastal Alaska, western coastal U.S. and Mexico

Food: mollusks, crustaceans, aquatic insects and plants

Compare: Larger than the female Black Scoter (p. 233), which has white cheeks and a smaller bill. Slightly larger than the female Surf Scoter (p. 235), which has a vertical white patch at the base of bill and white mark on nape.

Stan's Notes: Nests on the tundra in Alaska near freshwater lakes and ponds. Spends the winter at sea, rarely returning to shore. Sometimes in mixed flocks with other scoters. The genus name *Melanitta* from the Greek *melas* for "black" and *netta* for "duck" describes the bird well. The common name was first used in the Collective Catalogue of Birds (1674), but its origins are unknown.

male
p. 367

female

SUMMER

Canvasback
Aythya valisineria

Size: 20½" (52 cm)

Female: Brown head, neck and chest. Light-gray-to-brown sides. Long sloping forehead that transitions into a long dark bill.

Male: deep-red head and neck, sloping forehead, long black bill, gray-and-white sides and back, black chest and tail

Juvenile: similar to female

Nest: ground; female builds; 1 brood per year

Eggs: 7–9; pale white to gray without markings

Incubation: 24–29 days; female incubates

Fledging: 56–67 days; female leads young to food

Migration: complete, to western coastal states, Mexico

Food: aquatic insects, small clams

Compare: Female Greater Scaup (p. 217) and female Lesser Scaup (p. 199) are smaller, have a white marking at the base of their bills and lack the sloping forehead and long dark bill of the female Canvasback.

Stan's Notes: A large inland duck of freshwater lakes, rivers and ponds. Populations declined dramatically in the 1960–80s due to marsh drainage for agriculture. Females return to their birthplace (philopatric) while males disperse to new areas. Will mate during migration or on the breeding grounds. A courting male gives a soft cooing call when displaying and during aerial chases. Male leaves the female after incubation starts. Female takes a new mate every year. Female feeds very little during incubation and will lose up to 70 percent of fat reserves during that time.

239

male

female

YEAR-ROUND
SUMMER

Northern Pintail
Anas acuta

Size: 25" (63 cm), male
20" (52 cm), female

Male: A slender, elegant duck with a brown head, white neck and gray body. Gray bill. Extremely long and narrow black tail. Nonbreeding has a pale-brown head that lacks the clear demarcation between the brown head and white neck. Lacks long tail feathers.

Female: mottled brown body with a paler head and neck, long tail, gray bill

Juvenile: similar to female

Nest: ground; female builds; 1 brood per year

Eggs: 6–9; olive-green without markings

Incubation: 22–25 days; female incubates

Fledging: 36–50 days; female teaches young to feed

Migration: complete, to western coastal states, Mexico; non-migrator in parts of Alaska

Food: aquatic plants and insects, seeds

Compare: The male Northern Pintail has a distinctive brown head and white neck and unique long tail feathers. Female Mallard (p. 231) is similar to female Pintail, but Mallard has an orange bill with black spots.

Stan's Notes: A common dabbling duck of marshes. About 90 percent of its diet is aquatic plants, except when females feed heavily on aquatic insects prior to nesting, presumably to gain extra nutrients for egg production. Male holds tail upright from the water's surface. No other North American duck has such a long tail.

male
p. 329

female

soaring

Northern Harrier
Circus hudsonius

Size: 18–22" (45–56 cm); up to 4' wingspan

Female: Slender, low-flying hawk with a dark-brown back and brown streaking on the chest and belly. Large white rump patch. Thin black tail bands and black wing tips. Yellow eyes.

Male: silver-gray with a large white rump patch and white belly, black wing tips, yellow eyes, faint, thin bands across the tail

Juvenile: similar to female, with an orange breast

Nest: ground; female and male construct; 1 brood per year

Eggs: 4–8; bluish white without markings

Incubation: 31–32 days; female incubates

Fledging: 30–35 days; male and female feed the young

Migration: complete, to western states and Mexico

Food: mice, snakes, insects, small birds

Compare: Slimmer than the Red-tailed Hawk (p. 247). Look for the characteristic low gliding and the black tail bands to identify the female Harrier.

Stan's Notes: One of the easiest of hawks to identify. Glides just above the ground, following the contours of the land while searching for prey. Holds its wings just above horizontal, tilting back and forth in the wind, similar to the Turkey Vulture. Formerly called Marsh Hawk due to its habit of hunting over marshes. Feeds and nests on the ground. Will also preen and rest on the ground. Unlike other hawks, mainly uses its hearing to find prey, followed by its sight. At any age, it has a distinctive owl-like face disk.

243

juvenile

adult
soaring

juvenile
soaring

light
morph

juvenile

adult
soaring

juvenile
soaring

dark
morph

Rough-legged Hawk
Buteo lagopus

SUMMER
MIGRATION

Size: 18–23" (56 cm); up to 4½' wingspan

Male: A hawk of several plumages. All plumages have a long tail with a dark band or bands. Distinctive dark wrists and belly. Relatively long wings, small bill and feet. Light morph has nearly pure white undersides of wings and base of tail. Dark morph is nearly all brown with light-gray trailing edge of wings.

Female: same as male, only larger

Juvenile: same as adults

Nest: platform, on edge of cliff; female and male build; 1 brood per year

Eggs: 2–6; white without markings

Incubation: 28–31 days; female and male incubate

Fledging: 39–43 days; female and male feed young

Migration: complete, to the northern half of the U.S.

Food: small animals, snakes, large insects

Compare: Red-tailed Hawk (p. 247) has a belly band and lacks dark "wrist" marks. The Osprey (p. 97) has similar dark "wrists," but lacks the dark belly of the Rough-legged Hawk.

Stan's Notes: Two color morphs, light and dark, light being more common. A common summer resident and migrant in Alaska. Map reflects the combined range. More numerous in some years than others. It has much smaller and weaker feet than the other birds of prey, which means it must hunt smaller prey. Hunts from the air, usually hovering before diving for small rodents such as mice and voles.

Harlan's

soaring

Western

soaring

Red-tailed Hawk
Buteo jamaicensis

Size: 19–23" (48–63 cm); up to 4½' wingspan

Male: Variety of colorations, from chocolate brown to nearly all white. Often brown with a white breast and brown belly band. Rust-red tail. Underside of wing is white with a small dark patch on the leading edge near the shoulder.

Female: same as male but slightly larger

Juvenile: similar to adults, with a speckled breast and light eyes; lacks a red tail

Nest: platform; male and female build; 1 brood per year

Eggs: 2–3; white without markings or sometimes marked with brown

Incubation: 30–35 days; female and male incubate

Fledging: 45–46 days; male and female feed the young

Migration: complete, to western states and Mexico

Food: small and medium-sized animals, large birds, snakes, fish, insects, bats, carrion

Compare: Rough-legged Hawk (p. 245) has large, dark "wrist" marks, seen in flight.

Stan's Notes: A hawk of open country and cities, seen perching on freeway light posts, fences and trees. Look for it circling, searching for prey. Builds large stick nests in large trees along roads. Develops a red tail the second year. Harlan's is seen in the southern half of Alaska. Dark and light morphs. Map reflects the combined range.

YEAR-ROUND

Great Horned Owl
Bubo virginianus

Size: 21–25" (53–64 cm); up to 4' wingspan

Male: Robust brown "horned" owl. Bright-yellow eyes and a V-shaped white throat resembling a necklace. Horizontal barring on the chest.

Female: same as male but slightly larger

Juvenile: similar to adults but lacks ear tufts

Nest: no nest; takes over the nest of a crow, hawk or Great Blue Heron or uses a partial cavity, stump or broken tree; 1 brood per year

Eggs: 2–3; white without markings

Incubation: 26–30 days; female incubates

Fledging: 30–35 days; male and female feed the young

Migration: non-migrator

Food: mammals, birds (ducks), snakes, insects

Compare: Smaller than the Great Gray Owl (p. 337), which lacks ear tufts. Look for bright yellow eyes and feathers on head that look like horns to help identify the Great Horned.

Stan's Notes: One of the earliest nesting birds in the state, laying eggs in January and February. Able to hunt in complete darkness due to its excellent hearing. The "horns," or "ears," are tufts of feathers and have nothing to do with hearing. Cannot turn its head all the way around. Wing feathers are ragged on the ends, resulting in silent flight. Eyelids close from the top down, like humans. Fearless, it is one of the few animals that will kill skunks and porcupines. Given that, it is also called the Flying Tiger. Call sounds like "hoo-hoo-hoo-hoooo."

male
p. 349

female

Red-breasted Merganser

Mergus serrator

YEAR-ROUND
SUMMER

Size:	23" (58 cm)
Female:	Overall brown-to-gray duck with a shaggy reddish head and crest. Long orange bill.
Male:	shaggy green head and crest, a prominent white collar, rusty breast, black-and-white body, long orange bill
Juvenile:	similar to female
Nest:	ground; female builds; 1 brood per year
Eggs:	5–10; olive green without markings
Incubation:	29–30 days; female incubates
Fledging:	55–65 days; female feeds young
Migration:	complete to non-migrator in Alaska
Food:	fish, aquatic insects
Compare:	Smaller than female Common Merganser (p. 369), which has a rusty red head and larger orange bill

Stan's Notes: Breeding resident in Alaska. The most widespread of summer mergansers, arriving in April and leaving in October. Most commonly seen along the southeastern Alaska coast, but can also be seen in large inland freshwater lakes. This duck is a very fast flier, clocked at up to 100 miles (161 km) per hour. Frequently seen flying low across the water. Needs a long run for takeoff with wings flapping to get airborne. Serrated bill helps it catch slippery fish. Usually is a silent duck. Male sometimes gives a soft, catlike meow. Female gives a harsh "krrr-croak." Doesn't breed before 2 years of age. The male abandons the female just after eggs are laid. Females often share nests. The young leave the nest within 24 hours of hatching, never to return.

female

male
p. 99

Common Eider
Somateria mollissima

YEAR-ROUND
SUMMER
WINTER

Size: 24" (60 cm)

Female: Overall brown duck with a large body Long sloping forehead that leads into a large gray bill. White wing linings, seen in flight.

Male: black and white with a large body, short neck, black cap, dark eyes, forehead slopes into a large yellow bill, green wash to nape

Juvenile: similar to female

Nest: ground; female builds; 1 brood per year

Eggs: 3–6; pale green without markings

Incubation: 25–30 days; female incubates

Fledging: 65–75 days; female leads young to food

Migration: partial to non-migrator

Food: aquatic insects

Compare: The large size, unique shape and forehead sloping into a large yellow bill make this duck easy to identify.

Stan's Notes: This is our largest sea duck Found along the Pacific and Atlantic coasts. The western Arctic variety has a yellow bill, while the eastern variety has a green bill. Nests in small colonies on tundra ponds and rocky shores, usually within 100 feet (30 m) of water. Often prefers to nest on small islands that lack mammalian populations, especially Arctic Foxes. Mates may stay together for several years, but the male will leave the female shortly after she begins to incubate. Mothers usually don't eat while incubating, but leave to feed, regaining lost body fat after the young fledge. Two or three groups of ducklings gathered together (creches) are tended by 1–2 older females.

in flight

Greater White-fronted Goose
Anser albifrons

Size: 28" (71 cm); up to 4½' wingspan

Male: Grayish-brown bird with a distinctive white band at base of bill. Irregular black barring on the breast and belly. Bill is light pink to orange. Orange legs and feet. White rump and undertail.

Female: same as male

Juvenile: lighter color than adult and has yellowish legs, feet and bill

Nest: ground; female builds; 1 brood per year

Eggs: 4–7; creamy white without markings

Incubation: 23–25 days; female incubates

Fledging: 40–45 days; male and female teach young to feed

Migration: complete, to western coastal states, Mexico

Food: aquatic plants and insects

Compare: Similar size as the Snow Goose (p. 391). White morph Snow Goose is all white with black wing tips and a large, bright pink bill. Blue morph Snow Goose often has a white head and dark-gray body. Brant (p. 101) has a dark head, neck and white necklace.

Stan's Notes: Summer resident in parts of Alaska and seen during migration. Hybridizes with Snow and Canada Geese; often seen with them in mixed flocks or flying high up in large wedge shapes. Learns migratory route from parents and older members of flock. Doesn't breed until 3 years of age. Often called Speckle-belly by hunters due to the irregular marking on belly.

soaring

juvenile

juvenile

SUMMER

Golden Eagle
Aquila chrysaetos

Size: 30–40" (76–102 cm); up to 7¼' wingspan

Male: Uniform dark brown with a golden-yellow head and nape of neck. Yellow around base of bill. Yellow feet.

Female: same as male

Juvenile: similar to adult, with white "wrist" patches and a white base of tail

Nest: platform, on a cliff; female and male build; 1 brood per year

Eggs: 1–2; white with brown markings

Incubation: 43–45 days; female and male incubate

Fledging: 63–75 days; female and male feed young

Migration: complete, to western states and Mexico

Food: mammals, birds, reptiles, insects

Compare: The Bald Eagle (p. 105) adult is similar, but it has a white head and white tail. Bald Eagle juvenile is often confused with the Golden Eagle juvenile; both are large dark birds with white markings.

Stan's Notes: A large, powerful raptor that has no trouble taking larger prey such as jackrabbits. Hunts by perching or soaring and watching for movement. Inhabits mountainous terrain, requiring large territories to provide a large supply of food. Long-term pair bond, renewing its bond late in winter with spectacular high-flying courtship displays. Usually nests on cliff faces; rarely nests in trees. Uses a well-established nest that's been used for generations. Will add items to the nest such as antlers, bones and barbed wire.

SUMMER

Ruby-crowned Kinglet
Regulus calendula

Size: 4" (10 cm)

Male: Small, teardrop-shaped green-to-gray bird. Two white wing bars and a white eye-ring. Hidden ruby crown.

Female: same as male, but lacks a ruby crown

Juvenile: same as female

Nest: pendulous; female builds; 1 brood per year

Eggs: 4–5; white with brown markings

Incubation: 11–12 days; female incubates

Fledging: 11–12 days; female and male feed the young

Migration: complete, to western states, Mexico and Central America

Food: insects, berries

Compare: Golden-crowned Kinglet (p. 261) is similar, but its crown is yellow to orange. The Arctic Warbler (p. 265) is larger than the Ruby crowned Kinglet and has eyebrows.

Stan's Notes: One of the smaller birds in the state. Look for it flitting around thick, low shrubs. It takes a quick eye to see the ruby crown, which the male flashes when excited. The female weaves an unusually intricate nest and fastens colorful lichens and mosses to the exterior with spiderwebs. Often builds the nest high in a mature tree, hanging from a branch that has overlapping leaves. Sings a distinctive song that starts out soft and ends loud and on a higher note. "Kinglet" originates from the word king, referring to the male's red crown, and the diminutive suffix let, meaning "small."

male

female

Golden-crowned Kinglet

Regulus satrapa

YEAR-ROUND
SUMMER

Size: 4" (10 cm)

Male: Tiny, plump green-to-gray bird. Distinctive yellow-and-orange patch with a black border on the crown (see inset). A white eyebrow mark. Two white wing bars.

Female: same as male, but has a yellow crown with a black border, lacks any orange (see inset)

Juvenile: same as adults, but lacks gold on the crown

Nest: pendulous; female constructs; 1–2 broods per year

Eggs: 5–9; white or creamy with brown markings

Incubation: 14–15 days; female incubates

Fledging: 14–19 days; female and male feed young

Migration: non-migrator to partial in Alaska

Food: insects, fruit, tree sap

Compare: Similar to Ruby-crowned Kinglet (p. 259), but Golden-crowned has an obvious crown. Arctic Warbler (p. 265) is larger and lacks the black and yellowish crown.

Stan's Notes: Once considered a rare breeding bird in the state, it is now seen in parts of southern Alaska. While most migrate south, some stay and are commonly seen in winter. Often seen in flocks with chickadees, nuthatches, woodpeckers, Brown Creepers and Ruby-crowned Kinglets. Flicks its wings when moving around. Constructs an unusual hanging nest, often with moss, lichens and spiderwebs, and lines it with bark and feathers. Can have so many eggs in its small nest that eggs are in two layers. Drinks tree sap and feeds by gleaning insects from trees.

Red-breasted Nuthatch
Sitta canadensis

YEAR-ROUND

Size: 4½" (11 cm)

Male: Gray-backed bird with an obvious black eye line and black cap. Rust-red breast and belly.

Female: duller than male and has a gray cap and pale undersides

Juvenile: same as female

Nest: cavity; male and female excavate a cavity or move into a vacant hole; 1 brood per year

Eggs: 5–6; white with red-brown markings

Incubation: 11–12 days; female incubates

Fledging: 14–20 days; female and male feed the young

Migration: non-migrator to irruptive; moves around the state in search of food

Food: insects, insect eggs, seeds; comes to seed and suet feeders

Compare: Chestnut-backed Chickadee (p. 117) has brown on back and lacks eye line. Black-capped Chickadee (p. 267) lacks the rust-red breast and belly. Look for Red-breasted's rust-red breast and black eye line.

Stan's Notes: The nuthatch climbs down trunks of trees headfirst, searching for insects. Like a chickadee, it grabs a seed from a feeder and flies off to crack it open. Wedges the seed into a crevice and pounds it open with several sharp blows. The name "Nuthatch" comes from the Middle English moniker *nuthak*, referring to the habit of hacking seeds open. Look for it in mature conifers, where it extracts seeds from pine cones. Excavates a cavity or takes an old woodpecker hole or a natural cavity and builds a nest within. Gives a series of nasal "yank-yank-yank" calls.

Arctic Warbler
Phylloscopus borealis

SUMMER

Size: 5" (13 cm)

Male: Dull olive green-gray warbler. Long, narrow light line from the base of bill over each eye, extending nearly to the back of head. Small, very narrow wing bars. Bill is gray to dirty yellow. Pale yellow legs and feet.

Female: same as male

Juvenile: similar to adult

Nest: cup, with a dome covering (oven); female builds; 1 brood per year

Eggs: 4–7; pale white with reddish brown-to-pink markings

Incubation: 10–14 days; female incubates

Fledging: 18–20 days; female and male feed young

Migration: complete, to Philippines, East Indies, Asia

Food: insects

Compare: Ruby-crowned Kinglet (p. 259) is smaller and lacks eyebrows. The Golden-crowned Kinglet (p. 261) is also smaller and has a distinctive black and yellowish crown.

Stan's Notes: Actually a member of the Old World warbler group. Represents a diverse Eurasian group that reaches North America by crossing the Bering Sea to reach Alaska. Usually found along river banks in low, dense willow vegetation. Male perches and sings to attract a mate. Female uses dried grasses to build a unique dome shaped nest (oven) with an entrance hole on one side, and lines it with fine grass and animal hair. Often nests on the ground under a shrub. Feeds heavily on the abundant insects in Alaska in summer.

YEAR-ROUND

Black-capped Chickadee
Poecile atricapillus

Size: 5" (13 cm)

Male: Familiar gray bird with a black cap and throat patch. Tan sides and belly. White chest. Small white wing marks.

Female: same as male

Juvenile: same as adult

Nest: cavity; female and male excavate or use a nest box; 1 brood per year

Eggs: 5–7; white with fine brown markings

Incubation: 11–13 days; female and male incubate

Fledging: 14–18 days; female and male feed the young

Migration: non-migrator

Food: insects, seeds, fruit; comes to seed and suet feeders

Compare: Similar size as Boreal Chickadee (p. 269), which has a brown cap. Chestnut-backed Chickadee (p. 117) is similar in size, but has a distinctive chestnut back.

Stan's Notes: A perky backyard bird that can be attracted with a nest box or bird feeder. Usually the first to find a new seed or suet feeder. Can be easily tamed and hand fed. Much of the diet comes from bird feeders, so it can be a common urban bird. Needs to feed every day in winter and forages to find food even during the worst winter storms. Typically seen with nuthatches, woodpeckers and other birds. Builds nest mostly with green moss and lines it with fur. Named "Chickadee" for its familiar "chika-dee-dee-dee-dee" call. Also gives a high-pitched, two-toned "fee-bee" call. Can have different calls in different regions.

Boreal Chickadee

Poecile hudsonicus

YEAR-ROUND

Size: 5½" (14 cm)

Male: Overall gray with a brown cap, black chin, (bib) and light brown sides. White cheeks. Gray extending from cheeks toward nape.

Female: same as male

Juvenile: similar to adult

Nest: cavity; female and male excavate; 1 brood per year

Eggs: 5–8; pale white with brown markings

Incubation: 11–16 days; female incubates

Fledging: 16–18 days; female and male feed the young

Migration: non-migrator; moves around to find food

Food: seeds, insects; visits seed and suet feeders

Compare: Similar size as the Black-capped Chickadee (p. 267), which has a black cap. Chestnut-backed Chickadee (p. 117) is smaller than the Boreal Chickadee and has a distinctive chestnut back.

Stan's Notes: A common and widespread chickadee species in the southern two-thirds of Alaska. Like other chickadees, the Boreal is lightweight and has strong feet, allowing it to hang upside down to explore unexploited cracks and crevices for insects. Its wheezy call makes this bird easy to identify; even without seeing it.

female
p. 129

male

Dark-eyed Junco
Junco hyemalis

YEAR-ROUND
SUMMER
WINTER

Size: 5½" (14 cm)

Male: Plump, dark-eyed bird with a slate-gray-to-charcoal chest, head and back. White belly. Pink bill. White outer tail feathers appear like a white V in flight.

Female: round with brown plumage

Juvenile: similar to female, with streaking on the breast and head

Nest: cup; female and male build; 2 broods per year

Eggs: 3–5; white with reddish brown markings

Incubation: 12–13 days; female incubates

Fledging: 10–13 days; male and female feed the young

Migration: partial to complete migrator, throughout the U.S.

Food: seeds, insects; visits ground and seed feeders

Compare: Rarely confused with any other bird. Look for the pink bill and small flocks feeding under feeders to identify the male Dark-eyed Junco.

Stan's Notes: This is one of Alaska's common summer birds. Nests in a wide variety of wooded habitats in April and May. Adheres to a rigid social hierarchy, with dominant birds chasing the less dominant birds. Look for the white outer tail feathers flashing in flight. Often seen in small flocks on the ground, where it uses its feet to simultaneously "double-scratch" to expose seeds and insects. Eats many weed seeds. Several subspecies of Dark-eyed Junco were previously considered to be separate species.

male

female

SUMMER

Yellow-rumped Warbler
Setophaga coronata

Size: 5–6" (13–15 cm)

Male: Slate gray with black streaking on the chest. Yellow patches on the head, flanks and rump. White chin and belly. Two white wing bars.

Female: duller gray than the male, mixed with brown

Juvenile: first winter is similar to the adult female

Nest: cup; female builds; 2 broods per year

Eggs: 4–5; white with brown markings

Incubation: 12–13 days; female incubates

Fledging: 10–12 days; female and male feed young

Migration: complete, to western states, Mexico and Central America

Food: insects, berries; visits suet feeders in spring

Compare: Male Yellow Warbler (p. 401) is all yellow with orange streaks on the breast. The male Wilson's Warbler (p. 397) has a black cap.

Stan's Notes: A summer resident in most of Alaska, with flocks of hundreds seen during migration. Nests in coniferous and aspen forests. Familiar call is a single robust "chip," heard mostly during migration. Sings a wonderful song in spring. In the fall, the male molts to a dull color similar to the female, but he retains his yellow patches all year. Frequently called Audubon's Warbler in western states and Myrtle Warbler in eastern states. Sometimes called Butter-butt due to the yellow patch on its rump.

SUMMER

Bluethroat
Luscinia svecica

Size: 6" (15 cm)

Male: A gray bird with a bright blue chin, throat and upper breast. Rusty mark in center of throat and rust on the upper breast. White lower breast and belly. White eyebrows.

Female: similar to male, with less blue and a white chin and throat

Juvenile: similar to female, lacks blue and rust

Nest: cup; female and male construct; 1 brood per year

Eggs: 4–7; green with reddish brown markings

Incubation: 12–15 days; female incubates

Fledging: 10–14 days; female and male feed young

Migration: complete, to Southeast Asia, the Near East and Africa

Food: insects, seeds, berries

Compare: Male Northern Wheatear (p. 277) is the same size, but has a black mask and wings. Look for Bluethroat's blue and rust marks to identify.

Stan's Notes: Eurasian species found only in Alaska for the short summer months. Widely distributed in the Eurasian Arctic. Found in dense vegetation, where the male sings from prominent perches to attract a mate. Courting male throws its head back, cocks its tail and droop its wings while moving around the female and singing. Usually nests on the ground, constructing a cup nest of grass, roots, moss and lined with fine plant materials. Feeds mainly on insects. After the eggs hatch, both parents care for the young.

Northern Wheatear
Oenanthe oenanthe

Size: 6" (15 cm)

Male: A gray bird with black wings and tip of tail. Black mark through eyes, appearing like a mask. Tan mark near the side of the head, extending toward the upper breast. Nearly white belly White rump and undertail.

Female: similar to male, lacks the black mask

Juvenile: similar to female, lacks black wings

Nest: cavity; female and male construct; 1 brood per year

Eggs: 4–7; pale blue to white without markings

Incubation: 12–15 days; female and male incubate

Fledging: 15–16 days; female and male feed young

Migration: complete, to China, Mongolia, India, Africa

Food: insects, seeds, berries

Compare: Same size as the male Bluethroat (p. 275), which has a bright blue throat and upper breast. Look for the black mask and wings of male Northern Wheatear to help identify.

Stan's Notes: A Eurasian species seen only throughout Alaska and in parts of Canada in summer. Found in open tundra habitat with abundant rock piles or exposed cliffs. Nests in cavities underneath rocks, often in deserted mammal burrows. Builds nest from grass, roots and moss and lines it with fine plant material. Feeds mainly on insects. Male courts female by hopping and bowing around her with his tail fanned. Male will also sing a flight song before gliding down with tail fanned. Parents divide their brood 3–4 days after fledging, with each parent feeding its half of the young.

SUMMER

Western Wood-Pewee
Contopus sordidulus

Size: 6¼" (15.5 cm)

Male: An overall gray bird with darker wings and tail. Two narrow gray wing bars. Dull-white throat with pale-yellow or white belly. Black upper bill, dull-orange lower.

Female: same as male

Juvenile: similar to adult, lacking the two-toned bill

Nest: cup; female builds; 1 brood per year

Eggs: 2–4; pale white with brown markings

Incubation: 12–14 days; female incubates

Fledging: 14–18 days; female and male feed young

Migration: complete, to Central and South America

Food: insects

Compare: Say's Phoebe (p. 285) is larger and has a tawny belly.

Stan's Notes: Nesting bird in the southeastern quarter of the state. Breeds throughout western North America from Alaska to Mexico. Most common in aspen forests and places near water. It requires trees with dead tops or branches from which to sing and hunt for flying insects, which compose nearly all of the diet. Often returns to the same perch after each foray. Populations have been decreasing over recent years. Common name comes from its nasal whistle, "pee-wee."

breeding
p. 139

winter

SUMMER MIGRATION

Least Sandpiper
Calidris minutilla

Size: 6" (15 cm)

Male: Winter plumage is overall gray to light brown, with a distinct brown breast band and white belly. Light-gray eyebrows and short, thin, down-curved black bill. Dull-yellow legs.

Female: same as male

Juvenile: similar to winter adult, but buff-brown and lacks the breast band

Nest: ground; male and female construct; 1 brood per year

Eggs: 3–4; olive with dark markings

Incubation: 19–23 days; male and female incubate

Fledging: 25–28 days; male and female feed the young

Migration: complete, to California, Mexico and Central America

Food: aquatic and terrestrial insects, seeds

Compare: The smallest of sandpipers. Often confused with winter Western Sandpiper (p. 283). Least Sandpiper's yellow legs differentiate it from other tiny sandpipers. The short, thin, down-curved bill also helps to identify.

Stan's Notes: Seen in the southern three-quarters of the state in summer and during migration. This is a tiny, tame sandpiper that can be approached without scaring it. It is the smallest of peeps (sandpipers), nesting on the Alaskan tundra. Prefers the grassy flats of saltwater and freshwater ponds. Its yellow legs can be hard to see in water, poor light or when covered with mud. Most other small shorebirds have black legs and feet.

breeding
p. 143

winter

Western Sandpiper
Calidris mauri

SUMMER
MIGRATION

Size: 6½" (16 cm)

Male: Winter plumage is dull gray to light brown overall with a white belly and eyebrows. Black legs. Narrow bill that droops near tip.

Female: same as male

Juvenile: similar to breeding adult, bright buff-brown on the back only

Nest: ground; male and female construct; 1 brood per year

Eggs: 2–4; light brown with dark markings

Incubation: 20–22 days; male and female incubate

Fledging: 19–21 days; male and female feed the young

Migration: complete, to California, Mexico and Central America

Food: aquatic and terrestrial insects

Compare: Nonbreeding Least Sandpiper (p. 281) is very similar, but the Western Sandpiper has black legs and a longer bill that droops slightly at the tip. Nonbreeding Red Knot (p. 309) has barring on the flanks.

Stan's Notes: Summer resident along the western coast of Alaska, nesting on the tundra in large "loose" colonies. Adults leave their breeding grounds several weeks before the young. Feeds on insects at the water's edge, sometimes immersing its head. Young leave the nest (precocial) within a few hours after hatching. Female leaves and the male tends the hatchlings.

Say's Phoebe

Sayornis saya

SUMMER

Size: 7½" (19 cm)

Male: Overall dark gray, darkest on head, tail and wings. Belly and undertail tawny. Black bill.

Female: same as male

Juvenile: similar to adult, but browner overall with 2 tawny wing bars and a yellow lower bill

Nest: cup; female builds; 1–2 broods per year

Eggs: 3–6; pale white with brown markings

Incubation: 12–14 days; female incubates

Fledging: 14–16 days; female and male feed young

Migration: complete, to California, Mexico and Central and South America

Food: insects, berries

Compare: Western Wood-Pewee (p. 279) is smaller and lacks a tawny belly.

Stan's Notes: A widespread nester across Alaska below 9,000-foot (2,750 m) elevations. Nests in cliff crevices, abandoned buildings, bridges and other vertical structures. Frequently uses the same nest a couple of times in a season, returning the following year to that same nest. Has a nearly all-insect diet. Flies out from a perch to grab an aerial insect and returns to the same perch (hawking). Also hunts insects on the ground, hovering and dropping down to catch them. Phoebes are classified as New World Flycatchers and aren't related to Old World Flycatchers. Named after Thomas Say, who is said to have first recorded this bird in Colorado. The genus, species and first part of its common name refer to Mr. Say. Common name "Phoebe" is likely an imitation of the bird's call.

American Dipper
Cinclus mexicanus

YEAR-ROUND

Size: 7½" (19 cm)

Male: Dark gray to black overall. Head is slightly lighter in color. Short upturned tail. Dark eyes and bill.

Female: same as male

Juvenile: similar to adult, only paler with white eyelids that are most noticeable when blinking

Nest: pendulous, covered nest with the entrance near the bottom, on cliff, behind waterfall; female builds; 1–2 broods per year

Eggs: 3–5; white without markings

Incubation: 13–17 days; female incubates

Fledging: 18–25 days; female and male feed young

Migration: non-migrator; seeks moving open water in winter

Food: aquatic insects, small fish, crustaceans

Compare: American Robin (p. 299) is a similar shape, but it has a red breast. The only songbird in the state that dives into fast-moving water.

Stan's Notes: A common bird of fast, usually noisy streams that provide some kind of protected shelf on which to construct a nest. Some have had success attracting with man-made ledges. Plunges headfirst into fast-moving water, looking for just about any aquatic insect, propelling itself underwater with its wings. Frequently seen emerging with a large insect, which it smashes against rock before eating. Has the ability to fly directly into the air from underwater. Depending on snowmelt, nesting usually starts in March or April. Dippers in lower elevations often nest a second time each season.

juvenile

female

nonbreeding
male

male

Red-necked Phalarope
Phalaropus lobatus

Size: 8" (20 cm)

Female: Overall gray bird with a wide black stripe from base of bill across eyes and down the face. Rusty red neck. White chin and sides of body. Thin black bill. Long dark legs.

Male: similar to female, but duller and less red

Juvenile: similar to male, lacks the rusty red neck

Nest: ground; male builds; 1 brood per year

Eggs: 2–4; olive with brown markings

Incubation: 17–21 days; male incubates

Fledging: 18–21 days; male teaches young to feed

Migration: complete, to South America

Food: aquatic insects, seeds, crustaceans, mollusks

Compare: Smaller than the nonbreeding Short-billed Dowitcher (p. 307) and has a much shorter bill. Smaller than the breeding Red Knot (p. 309), which has a rusty red neck, chest and belly.

Stan's Notes: Female is brighter than male, and the sex roles are reversed. Some females mate with many males (polyandrous) and lay eggs. Female abandons male once eggs are laid. Male builds a ground nest along tundra ponds, often under a low shrub, and lines it with grass and moss. Male incubates with a brood patch, a bare area on the belly that keeps eggs close to the body for incubation, something only females usually have. Young hatch at the same time and swim within hours of birth. Males often adopt orphans. Doesn't dive underwater to feed, but swims about like a wind-up toy, often spinning in circles, quickly picking up insects stirred to the surface.

breeding
p. 159

winter

SUMMER MIGRATION

Dunlin
Calidris alpina

Size: 8–9" (20–23 cm)

Male: Winter adult has a brownish-gray back with a light-gray chest and white belly. Stout bill curves slightly downward at tip. Black legs.

Female: slightly larger than the male, with a longer bill

Juvenile: slightly rusty back with a spotty chest

Nest: ground; male and female construct; 1 brood per year

Eggs: 2–4; olive-buff or blue-green with red-brown markings

Incubation: 21–22 days; male incubates during the day, female incubates at night

Fledging: 19–21 days; male feeds the young, female often leaves before the young fledge

Migration: complete, to western coastal U.S., Mexico and Central America

Food: insects

Compare: Winter Dunlin has a stout down-turned bill and is overall gray.

Stan's Notes: Usually seen in gray winter plumage from August to early May. Breeding plumage is more commonly seen in the spring. Flights include heights of up to 100 feet (30 m) with brief gliding alternating with shallow flutters, and a rhythmic, repeating song. Huge flocks fly synchronously, with birds twisting and turning, flashing light and dark undersides. Males tend to fly farther south in winter than females. Doesn't nest in the state.

Townsend's Solitaire
Myadestes townsendi

SUMMER

Size: 8½" (22 cm)

Male: All-gray robin look-alike. Prominent white ring around each eye. Wings slightly darker than the body. Long tail. Short dark bill. Dark legs.

Female: same as male

Juvenile: darker gray with a tan scaly appearance

Nest: cup; female builds; 1–2 broods per year

Eggs: 3–5; blue, green, gray or white with brown markings

Incubation: 12–14 days; female incubates

Fledging: 10–14 days; female and male feed young

Migration: complete, to southwestern states, Mexico; known to migrate to eastern states

Food: insects, fruit

Compare: American Robin (p. 299) has a red breast. Canada Jay (p. 315) has a white head.

Stan's Notes: A summer resident of coniferous mountain forests. "Hawks" for insects, perching in trees and darting out to capture them. Eats berries in winter when insects are not available and actively defends a good berry source from other birds. Builds nest on ground sheltered by rocks or an overhang, or sometimes low in a tree or shrub. Song is a series of clear flute-like whistles without a distinct pattern. Shows white outer tail feathers and light tan patches on wings when in flight.

male
p. 29

female

SUMMER

Rusty Blackbird
Euphagus carolinus

Size: 9" (23 cm)

Female: Overall gray blackbird with rusty edges of feathers. Yellow eyes. A short, thin pointed bill. Nonbreeding is much browner with a gray rump and black patch around each eye.

Male: glossy black blackbird with blue and purple highlights, bright yellow eyes, a short, thin pointed bill, nonbreeding plumage is more rusty brown than glossy black

Juvenile: similar to female

Nest: cup; female builds; 1–2 broods per year

Eggs: 4–5; bluish with brown markings

Incubation: 12–14 days; female incubates

Fledging: 11–13 days; female and male feed young

Migration: complete, to lower 48 states

Food: insects, seeds

Compare: Female Red-winged Blackbird (p. 163) is slightly smaller and heavily streaked, with prominent white eyebrows.

Stan's Notes: This bird nests across most of Alaska in small loose colonies, often preferring more wooded, swampy areas. Male feeds female while she incubates. Gathers in large groups. Flocks with other blackbirds to migrate in autumn. When in flight, the end of tail often appears squared.

male
p. 361

female

Pine Grosbeak
Pinicola enucleator

YEAR-ROUND
SUMMER

Size: 9" (23 cm)

Female: Plump gray finch with a long dark tail. Dark wings with two white wing bars. Head and rump have a dull-yellow tinge. Short, pointed dark bill.

Male: plump bird, overall rose-red and gray

Juvenile: female is similar to the adult female; male has a touch of red on the head and rump

Nest: cup; female builds; 1 brood per year

Eggs: 4–5; bluish green without markings

Incubation: 13–15 days; female incubates

Fledging: 13–20 days; female and male feed the young

Migration: partial to non-migrator to irruptive; moves around in winter to find food

Food: seeds, fruit, insects; will come to seed feeders

Compare: Female Red Crossbill (p. 405) and female White-winged Crossbill (p. 407) are much smaller and have a crossed bill.

Stan's Notes: This winter finch is common in Alaska in some years and not so common in others. A very tame and approachable seed eater. Often seen along roads or on the ground, eating tiny grains of sand and dirt, which help aid digestion. Favors coniferous woods, rarely moving out of coniferous regions during summer, but also likes mixed forests. Will bathe in fluffy snow. Flies in a typical finch-like undulating pattern while giving soft, whistle "cheer" calls. Male sings a rich, beautiful song all year long. Male and female develop a pouch in the bottom of their mouths (buccal pouch) during the breeding season for transporting seeds to their young.

male

female

SUMMER

American Robin
Turdus migratorius

Size: 9–11" (23–28 cm)

Male: Familiar gray bird with a dark rust-red breast and a nearly black head and tail. White chin with black streaks. White eye-ring.

Female: similar to male, with a duller rust-red breast and a gray head

Juvenile: similar to female, with a speckled breast and brown back

Nest: cup; female builds with help from the male; 2–3 broods per year

Eggs: 4–7; pale blue without markings

Incubation: 12–14 days; female incubates

Fledging: 14–16 days; female and male feed the young

Migration: complete, to western states, Mexico and Central America

Food: insects, fruit, berries, earthworms

Compare: Familiar bird to all. To differentiate the male from the female, compare the nearly black head and rust-red chest of the male with the gray head and duller chest of the female.

Stan's Notes: Can be heard singing all night long in spring. City robins sing louder than country robins in order to hear one another over traffic and noise. A robin isn't listening for worms when it turns its head to one side. It is focusing its sight out of one eye to look for dirt moving, which is caused by worms moving. Territorial, often fighting its reflection in a window. Males have dark heads and a brighter red breast than females.

Northern Shrike
Lanius borealis

YEAR-ROUND
SUMMER
WINTER

Size: 10" (25 cm)

Male: Overall gray bird with black wings and tail. Distinctive black mask across eyes. A small white patch on black wings, seen in flight. Large black bill with a hooked tip.

Female: same as male

Juvenile: tan to light brown overall with dark wings, finely streaked chest

Nest: cup; female and male construct; 1 brood per year

Eggs: 4–6; gray to olive green with brown marks

Incubation: 15–16 days; female incubates

Fledging: 18–20 days; male and female feed young

Migration: complete to non-migrator, to southeastern Alaska and northern states

Food: large insects, small mammals, small birds

Compare: Canada Jay (p. 315) is larger and lacks the black mask and wings. Look for the black mask and large black bill with a hooked tip to help identify the Northern Shrike.

Stan's Notes: Songbird that acts like a bird of prey. Often seen out in the open, where it sits still for long periods of time watching for prey movement. Unlike a bird of prey; its feet aren't strong enough to hold prey still while it eats. Skewers large insects, mice and other prey on barbed wire fences, long thorns or other sharp objects to hold prey still while tearing it apart. For this reason, it is also called Butcher Bird. Winter populations and migratory behavior may be influenced by the availability of food.

breeding

winter

Surfbird

Calidris virgata

SUMMER
MIGRATION
WINTER

Size: 10" (25 cm)

Male: Breeding (Mar–Aug) is gray with dark spots and a tan-to-brown wash on upper wings and back. White belly. Yellow legs and feet. Winter Jul–Apr) is gray with a white belly. Distinctive black-tipped white tail. White wing linings, seen in flight anytime of year.

Female: same as male

Juvenile: similar to winter adult

Nest: ground; female and male construct; 1 brood per year

Eggs: 1–4; pale tan with brown markings

Incubation: 22–24 days; female and male incubate

Fledging: 19–24 days; female and male feed young

Migration: complete, to southeastern coastal Alaska, western coastal U.S. and Mexico

Food: aquatic insects, mussels, barnacles, seeds, crustaceans

Compare: Slightly larger than the breeding Ruddy Turnstone (p. 59), which has a black and white face. The breeding Red Knot (p. 363) has a salmon head, chest and belly.

Stan's Notes: Nests along rocky alpine ridges above the tree line in Alaska. Winters in small flocks of under 20 individuals. Feeding birds give high squeaks to keep in contact with the flock. Usually difficult for people to hear these birds due to loud crashing surf. Has three different breeding vocalizations: songs, calls and laughs. Male performs display flights of long gliding phases while calling.

soaring

juvenile

Sharp-shinned Hawk
Accipiter striatus

YEAR-ROUND
SUMMER

Size: 10–14" (25–36 cm); up to 2' wingspan

Male: Small woodland hawk with a gray back and head and a rust-red chest. Short wings. Long, squared tail and several dark tail bands, with the widest at the end of the tail. Red eyes.

Female: same as male but larger

Juvenile: same size as adults, with a brown back, heavy streaking on the chest and yellow eyes

Nest: platform; female builds; 1 brood per year

Eggs: 4–5; white with brown markings

Incubation: 32–35 days; female incubates

Fledging: 24–27 days; female and male feed the young

Migration: complete to non-migrator in Alaska

Food: birds, small mammals

Compare: Much smaller than the Northern Goshawk (p. 333), which has distinctive white eye brows. Look for the Sharp-shinned Hawks squared tail to help identify.

Stan's Notes: A hawk of backyards, parks and woodlands. Seen swooping on birds visiting feeders and chasing them as they flee. Its short wingspan and long tail help it to maneuver through thick stands of trees in pursuit of prey. Calls a loud, high-pitched "kik-kik-kik-kik." Named "Sharp-shinned" for the sharp projection (keel) on the leading edge of its shin. A bird's shin is actually below the ankle (rather than above it, like ours) on the tarsus bone of its foot. In most birds, the tarsus bone is rounded, not sharp.

winter

breeding
p. 173

Short-billed Dowitcher

Limnodromus griseus

SUMMER
MIGRATION

Size: 11" (28 cm)

Male: Winter plumage back and wings are gray to light brown and the belly is white. Has a long, straight black bill. Off-white eyebrow stripe. Dull-yellow-to-green legs and feet.

Female: same as male

Juvenile: similar to winter adult

Nest: ground; female and male construct; 1 brood per year

Eggs: 3–4; olive-green with dark markings

Incubation: 20–21 days; male and female incubate

Fledging: 25–27 days; male and female feed the young

Migration: complete, to coastal Mexico

Food: insects, snails, worms, leeches, seeds

Compare: Nonbreeding Black-bellied Plover (p. 313) is similar in size, but has a tiny bill unlike the long bill of the Short-billed Dowitcher. The nonbreeding Red Knot (p. 309) lacks the dark patch on head and has a shorter bill. Red-necked Phalarope (p. 289) is smaller and has a much shorter bill.

Stan's Notes: Summer resident seen along southern coastal Alaska and inland on freshwater lakes and marshes. With a rapid probing action like a sewing machine, it uses its long straight bill to probe deep into sand and mud for insects.

nonbreeding

breeding
p. 363

Red Knot
Calidris canutus

SUMMER MIGRATION

Size: 11" (28 cm)

Male: Nonbreeding (Sep–Apr) is overall gray with dark wing tips and dark barring on white flanks. Medium length straight black bill.

Female: same as male

Juvenile: overall gray with white eyebrows and dull yellow legs

Nest: ground; male and female construct; 1 brood per year

Eggs: 3–4; olive with brown markings

Incubation: 21–23 days; male and female incubate

Fledging: 18–20 days; female and male feed young

Migration: complete, to coastal California, Mexico and Central and South America

Food: insects, mollusks, snails, marine worms, small fish

Compare: The nonbreeding Short-billed Dowitcher (p. 307) has a longer bill, dark patch on head and feeds by probing into mud like a sewing machine. The nonbreeding Western Sandpiper (p. 283) lacks barring on flanks.

Stan's Notes: One of the longest migrating shorebirds, nesting on the Arctic tundra and wintering as far south as Tierra del Fuego, Argentina. Stops in coastal North America. Feeds in large flocks of up to 100 individuals, often with other shorebirds. Usually is seen standing on one leg on the beach, resting between feedings. Was the most abundant shorebird in North America; hunting in the late 1800s to early 1900s severely reduced the overall population.

breeding
p. 63

nonbreeding

American Golden-Plover
Pluvialis dominica

SUMMER MIGRATION

Size: 11" (28 cm)

Male: Nonbreeding plumage (Sep–Apr) is overall gray with white eyebrows and a dark cap. Short dark bill.

Female: same as nonbreeding male

Juvenile: similar to nonbreeding adult

Nest: ground; male builds; 1 brood per year

Eggs: 3–4; cream with brown markings

Incubation: 26–28 days; male and female incubate

Fledging: 20–22 days; male and female show young what to eat

Migration: complete, to South America

Food: insects, fruit, seeds

Compare: Nonbreeding Black-bellied Plover (p. 313) is similar in size, but has less distinct white eyebrows and a white undertail

Stan's Notes: This bird was formerly called Lesser Golden-Plover. Was once hunted by market hunters. More than 48,000 birds were reported to have been shot in one day near New Orleans in 1861. Populations were extremely depleted by the early 1900s. May mate for life. Male does most of the nest selection and construction. Male also incubates most of the time. Both sexes feed the young equally.

breeding
p. 65

winter

Black-bellied Plover
Pluvialis squatarola

SUMMER
MIGRATION

Size: 11–12" (28–30 cm)

Male: Winter plumage is uniform light gray with a white belly and breast. Faint white eyebrow mark. Black legs and bill.

Female: less black on belly and breast than male

Juvenile: grayer than adults, with much less black

Nest: ground; male and female construct; 1 brood per year

Eggs: 3–4; pink or green with black-brown markings

Incubation: 26–27 days; male incubates during the day, female incubates at night

Fledging: 35–45 days; male feeds the young, the young learn quickly to feed themselves

Migration: complete, to coastal California and Mexico

Food: insects

Compare: Nonbreeding American Golden-Plover (p. 311) lacks the white undertail. The non-breeding Spotted Sandpiper (p. 157) has a shorter, thicker bill.

Stan's Notes: Males perform a "butterfly" courtship flight to attract females. Female leaves male and young about 12 days after the eggs hatch. Breeds at age 3. Migrant and summer resident along coastal Alaska. During flight, in any plumage, displays a white rump and stripe on wings with black axillaries (armpits). Often darts across the ground to grab an insect and run.

Canada Jay
Perisoreus canadensis

YEAR-ROUND

Size: 11½" (29 cm)

Male: Large gray bird with a white forehead and nape of neck. Short black bill. Dark eyes.

Female: same as male

Juvenile: sooty gray with a faint white whisker mark

Nest: cup; male and female construct; 1 brood per year

Eggs: 3–4; gray white, finely marked to unmarked

Incubation: 16–18 days; female incubates

Fledging: 14–15 days; male and female feed young

Migration: non-migrator; moves around to find food in winter

Food: insects, seeds, fruit, nuts; visits seed feeders

Compare: Slightly larger than the Steller's Jay (p. 113), but lacks any blue coloring and a crest. The Northern Shrike (p. 301) is smaller and has a black mask and wings.

Stan's Notes: A bird of coniferous woods in mid to high elevations. Called Camp Robber because it rummages through camps looking for scraps of food. Also known as Whisky Jack or Gray Jay. Easily tamed, it will fly to your hand if offered raisins or nuts. Will eat just about anything. Also stores extra food for winter, balling it together in a sticky mass, placing it on a tree limb, often concealing it with lichen or bark. Travels around in family units of 3–5, making good companions for campers, canoeists and high altitude hikers and climbers. Reminds some of an overgrown chickadee.

Eurasian Collared-Dove
Streptopelia decaocto

Size: 12½" (32 cm)

Male: Head, neck, breast and belly are gray to tan. Back, wings and tail are slightly darker. Thin black collar with a white border on the nape of the neck. Tail is long and squared.

Female: same as male

Juvenile: similar to adults

Nest: platform; female and male build; 2–3 broods per year

Eggs: 3–5; creamy white without markings

Incubation: 12–14 days; female and male incubate

Fledging: 12–14 days; female and male feed the young

Migration: non-migrator

Food: seeds; will visit ground and seed feeders

Compare: The Rock Pigeon (p. 319) has colorful iridescent patches. Look for the black collar on the nape and the squared tail to help identify the Eurasian Collared-Dove.

Stan's Notes: This non-native bird has spread into the Lower 48 states from Florida in the early 1980s after inadvertent introduction to the Bahamas. It has been expanding its range across North America and is predicted to spread just like it did through Europe from Asia. Unknown how this "new" bird will affect populations of the native Mourning Dove. Nearly identical to the Ringed Turtle-Dove, a common pet bird. The dark mark on the back of the neck gave rise to the common name. Look for flashes of white in the tail and dark wing tips when it lands or takes off.

Rock Pigeon
Columba livia

YEAR-ROUND

Size: 13" (33 cm)

Male: No set color pattern. Shades of gray to white with patches of gleaming, iridescent green and blue. Often has a light rump patch.

Female: same as male

Juvenile: same as adults

Nest: platform; female builds; 3–4 broods per year

Eggs: 1–2; white without markings

Incubation: 18–20 days; female and male incubate

Fledging: 25–26 days; female and male feed the young

Migration: non-migrator

Food: seeds

Compare: The Eurasian Collared-Dove (p. 317) has a black collar on the nape.

Stan's Notes: Also known as the Domestic Pigeon. Formerly known as the Rock Dove. Introduced to North America from Europe by the early settlers. Most common around cities and barnyards, where it scratches for seeds. One of the few birds with a wide variety of colors, produced by years of selective breeding while in captivity. Parents feed the young a regurgitated liquid known as crop-milk for the first few days of life. One of the few birds that can drink without tilting its head back. Nests under bridges or on buildings, balconies, barns and sheds. Was once thought to be a nuisance in cities and was poisoned. Now, many cities have Peregrine Falcons (p. 327) feeding on Rock Pigeons, which keeps their numbers in check.

in flight

SUMMER
MIGRATION

Long-tailed Jaeger
Stercorarius longicaudus

Size: 15" (38 cm); 8" tail; up to 3½' wingspan

Male: A gray bird with darker gray wings and tail. Black cap, nearly white head and short dark bill. Gray legs. Breeding plumage has an extremely long, thin tail.

Female: same as male

Juvenile: dark brown overall with a black-tipped bill

Nest: ground; female and male construct; 1 brood per year

Eggs: 1–2; olive to brown with brown markings

Incubation: 23–25 days; female and male incubate

Fledging: 22–28 days; female and male feed young

Migration: complete, to South America

Food: small mammals and birds, insects, berries

Compare: Parasitic Jaeger (p. 323) has a brown cap, shorter tail and slightly larger body. Long tailed is similar in size and shape to many juvenile gulls, but has a black cap. Look for the very long tail to help identify.

Stan's Notes: One of several jaeger species in Alaska. The smallest of the jaegers but has the longest tail, hence its common name. The long tail feathers are molted and replaced with shorter ones for the winter. The nesting biology of all jaeger species is very similar. Has a long-term pair bond, returning to the same region yearly to nest. A ground nester that will actively defend its nest site from intruders, including large mammals. Male defends territory and hunts. Female does most of the incubation and brooding after the eggs hatch.

in flight

Parasitic Jaeger
Stercorarius parasiticus

Size: 16½" (42 cm); 4" tail; up to 3½' wingspan

Male: A gray bird with darker gray wings, tail and legs. A pale yellow-to-white head and neck with a dark brown cap. Short dark bill with a white base. Narrow pointed tail. Small white patch near wing tips, as seen in flight.

Female: same as male

Juvenile: dark brown overall, a black-tipped gray bill

Nest: ground; female and male construct; 1 brood per year

Eggs: 1–2; olive to brown with brown markings

Incubation: 23–28 days; female and male incubate

Fledging: 25–30 days; female and male feed young

Migration: complete, to coastal California, Mexico and Central and South America

Food: birds, eggs, fish, mammals, insects, berries

Compare: Long-tailed Jaeger (p. 321) has a black cap and longer tail. Juvenile Parasitic Jaeger has a similar size and shape as many juvenile gulls, but has a brown cap. Look for short, pointed central tail feathers and a flash of white near the wing tips when in flight.

Stan's Notes: Often the most common of the jaegers. Usually seen near the coast. Moves out to sea during migration, where it often steals fish from other bird species. Diet is mainly young birds and bird eggs. Sometimes follows predators such as wolves, snatching birds that are distracted by the predator. Has a long-term pair bond.

female
p. 225

male

Gadwall
Mareca strepera

YEAR-ROUND
SUMMER

Size: 19" (48 cm)

Male: A plump gray duck with a brown head and a distinctive black rump. White belly. Chestnut-tinged wings. Bright-white wing linings. Small white wing patch, seen when swimming. Gray bill.

Female: similar to female Mallard, a mottled brown with a pronounced color change from dark-brown body to light-brown neck and head, bright-white wing linings, small white wing patch, gray bill with orange sides

Juvenile: similar to female

Nest: ground; female lines the nest with fine grass and down feathers plucked from her chest; 1 brood per year

Eggs: 8–11; white without markings

Incubation: 24–27 days; female incubates

Fledging: 48–56 days; young feed themselves

Migration: partial to non-migrator in Alaska

Food: aquatic plants and insects

Compare: Male Gadwall is one of the few gray ducks. Look for its distinctive black rump.

Stan's Notes: A duck of shallow marshes. Consumes mostly plant material, dunking its head in water to feed rather than tipping forward, like other dabbling ducks. Walks well on land; feeds in fields and woodlands. Frequently in pairs with other duck species. Nests within 300 feet (90 m) of water. Establishes pair bond in winter.

juvenile

in-flight
juvenile

in flight

Peregrine Falcon
Falco peregrinus

YEAR-ROUND
SUMMER
MIGRATION

Size: 16–20" (41–51 cm); up to 3¾' wingspan

Male: Dark-gray back and tan-to-white chest. Horizontal bars on belly, legs and undertail. Dark "hood" head marking and wide black mustache. Yellow base of bill and eye-ring. Yellow legs.

Female: similar to male but noticeably larger

Juvenile: overall darker than adults, with heavy streaking on the chest and belly

Nest: ground (scrape) on a cliff edge, tall building, bridge or smokestack; 1 brood per year

Eggs: 3–4; white, some with brown markings

Incubation: 29–32 days; female and male incubate

Fledging: 35–42 days; male and female feed the young

Migration: complete to non-migrator in Alaska

Food: birds (Rock Pigeons in cities, shorebirds and waterfowl in rural areas)

Compare: The American Kestrel (p. 167) is smaller and has 2 vertical black stripes on its face. Look for the dark "hood" head marking and mustache marks to identify the Peregrine Falcon.

Stan's Notes: A wide-bodied raptor that hunts many bird species. Lives in many cities, diving (stooping) on pigeons at speeds of up to 200 miles (322 km) per hour, which knocks them to the ground. Soars with its wings flat, often riding thermals. During courtship, the male brings food to the female and performs aerial displays. Likes to nest on a high ledge or platform for a good view of its territory. A solitary nester and monogamous. Found throughout most of Alaska.

male

female
p. 243

soaring

SUMMER

Northern Harrier
Circus hudsonius

Size: 18–22" (45–56 cm); up to 4' wingspan

Male: Slender, low-flying hawk. Silver-gray with a large white rump patch and white belly. Long tail with faint narrow bands. Black wing tips. Yellow eyes.

Female: dark-brown back, brown streaking on breast and belly, large white rump patch, thin black tail bands, black wing tips, yellow eyes

Juvenile: similar to female, with an orange breast

Nest: ground; female and male construct; 1 brood per year

Eggs: 4–8; bluish white without markings

Incubation: 31–32 days; female incubates

Fledging: 30–35 days; male and female feed the young

Migration: complete, to western states and Mexico

Food: mice, snakes, insects, small birds

Compare: Slimmer than the Red-tailed Hawk (p. 247). Look for a low-gliding hawk with a large white rump patch to identify the male Harrier.

Stan's Notes: One of the easiest of hawks to identify. Glides just above the ground, following the contours of the land while searching for prey. Holds its wings just above horizontal, tilting back and forth in the wind, similar to Turkey Vultures. Formerly called the Marsh Hawk due to its habit of hunting over marshes. Feeds and nests on the ground. Will also preen and rest on the ground. Unlike other hawks, mainly uses its hearing to find prey, followed by sight. At any age, has a distinctive owl-like face disk.

in flight

juvenile

Gyrfalcon
Falco rusticolus

YEAR-ROUND
WINTER

Size: 20–25" (51–64 cm); up to 4' wingspan

Male: Largest falcon worldwide. Light gray head, back and tail. Dark horizontal barring on a pale white breast and belly. Back and wings have black horizontal barring. Yellow base of bill, eye-rings and legs.

Female: similar to male, noticeably larger

Juvenile: overall light brown with streaking through out, has two-toned underwings with a paler trailing edge, a wider, longer tail than the adults, bluish cere, eye-rings and legs

Nest: no nest, scrape in dirt on the edge of a cliff; 1 brood per year

Eggs: 3–5; white with brown markings

Incubation: 34–36 days; female and male incubate

Fledging: 49–56 days; male and female feed young

Migration: non-migrator to partial

Food: birds (mainly ptarmigan), small mammals

Compare: Peregrine Falcon (p. 327) is smaller, has a black "hood" and narrower, more pointed wings with darker underwings.

Stan's Notes: A non-migrator and winter resident in Alaska, with some moving farther south in late autumn and winter. Seen only infrequently. Hunts by flying low and capturing prey by surprise. Soars with wings flat. Breeds on rock outcrops in the Arctic tundra. May skip nesting when prey is scarce. The smaller male does most of the hunting during incubation.

in flight

juvenile

juvenile
in flight

YEAR-ROUND

Northern Goshawk
Accipiter gentilis

Size: 21–26" (53–66 cm); up to 3½' wingspan

Male: Blue gray back and upper wings. Light gray breast and belly. Gray underwings with fine dark barring. Black crown. Prominent white eyebrows. Eyes are deep red to mahogany. White undertail coverts. Yellow feet.

Female: similar to male, noticeably larger, barring on the breast is more coarse

Juvenile: overall streaked brown with irregular dark bands on tail, yellow eyes

Nest: platform, in a tree; male and female build; 1 brood per year

Eggs: 2–5; bluish white, sometimes brown marks

Incubation: 36–38 days; female and male incubate

Fledging: 35–42 days; male and female feed young

Migration: non-migrator to irruptive, to northern states

Food: birds (especially grouse), small mammals

Compare: Much larger than the Sharp-shinned Hawk (p. 305), which has a rusty chest. Look for the gray chest and white undertail coverts of the Northern Goshawk.

Stan's Notes: This is the largest of our woodland accipiters. Hunts by chasing or surprising. Highly dependent on Ruffed Grouse for food; goshawk populations follow grouse populations. Breeds in parts of the lower two-thirds of Alaska, usually beginning at 3 years of age. Female is very aggressive at the nest, boldly attacking. The smaller male hunts smaller prey and feeds the incubating female. Juveniles migrate first.

winter

breeding

YEAR-ROUND
SUMMER

Red-throated Loon
Gavia stellata

Size: 25" (63 cm)

Male: Breeding (Apr–Oct) is overall dark brown to nearly black with a gray head and neck and prominent red throat. Long, thin black bill. Winter (Oct–Apr) lacks the red throat, has a white face, neck and breast and a gray back with white spots.

Female: same as male

Juvenile: similar to winter adult

Nest: platform, on the ground; male and female build; 1 brood per year

Eggs: 1–3; brown to olive without markings

Incubation: 24–29 days; female and male incubate

Fledging: 49–51 days; male and female feed young

Migration: complete to non-migrator in Alaska

Food: fish, aquatic insects, amphibians

Compare: Smaller than the breeding Common Loon (p. 103), which has a black head, a larger, wider bill and lacks the red throat. Winter Common Loon has less white on the neck and face than winter Red-throated Loon.

Stan's Notes: The smallest of loons and the only one that can take flight from dry land rather than by running on the water's surface. Nests on smaller lakes and ponds. Often lays two eggs. Young hatch up to several days apart and ride on backs of swimming adults for their first couple weeks. Less vocal than Common Loon, but gives a short wailing call on breeding grounds. Groups of up to 100 may gather to feed at summers end; smaller groups migrate during days.

in flight

YEAR-ROUND

Great Gray Owl
Strix nebulosa

Size: 27" (69 cm); up to 4' wingspan

Male: Overall gray owl with a large, round puffy head and large, light gray facial disk with a thin black outline. Black and white throat, resembling a bow tie. Yellow eyes.

Female: same as male, only slightly larger

Juvenile: similar to adults, light gray

Nest: platform; takes over a crow or hawk nest or uses a stump or broken-off tree; 1 brood per year

Eggs: 2–4; white without markings

Incubation: 28–30 days; female incubates

Fledging: 21–28 days; male and female feed young

Migration: non-migrator to irruptive; moves around Alaska in winter to find food

Food: small to medium mammals

Compare: Great Horned Owl (p. 249) is smaller and has ear tufts.

Stan's Notes: Our largest owl. Nests in the southeastern quarter of Alaska. Detects prey beneath snow by sound, plunging into snow to capture. Often hunts along roads during winter to capture mice that have left the cover of snow. This leads to many owl-and-car collisions. One of the more active owls during the day. Not often frightened by human presence. During courtship, male gives 5–10 deep hoots. Female responds with a low whistle or hoot. Some use an artificial nest platform. Young will return to roost in the nest.

in flight

Canada Goose
Branta canadensis

SUMMER
MIGRATION

Size: 25–43" (64–109 cm); up to 5½' wingspan

Male: Large gray goose with a black neck and head. White chin and cheek strap.

Female: same as male

Juvenile: same as adults

Nest: platform, on the ground; female builds; 1 brood per year

Eggs: 5–10; white without markings

Incubation: 25–30 days; female incubates

Fledging: 42–55 days; male and female teach the young to feed

Migration: complete, to western states

Food: aquatic plants, insects, seeds

Compare: Similar size as the Brant (p. 101), which has a white necklace and lacks Canada Goose's white cheek strap.

Stan's Notes: Summer resident in most of Alaska and seen during migration. Calls a classic "honk-honk-honk," especially in flight. Flocks fly in a large V when traveling long distances. Begins breeding in the third year. Adults mate for many years. If threatened, they will hiss as a warning. Males stand as sentinels at the edge of their group and will bob their heads and become aggressive if approached. Adults molt their primary flight feathers while raising their young, rendering family groups temporarily flightless. Several subspecies vary in the U.S. Generally eastern groups are paler than western. Their size also varies, decreasing northward. The smallest subspecies is in the Arctic.

in flight

rusty stain

in-flight rusty stain

Sandhill Crane

Grus canadensis

Size: 42–48" (107–122 cm); up to 7' wingspan

Male: Elegant gray crane with long legs and neck. Wings and body often rust brown from mud staining. Scarlet-red cap. Yellow to red eyes.

Female: same as male

Juvenile: dull brown with yellow eyes; lacks a red cap

Nest: ground; female and male construct; 1 brood per year

Eggs: 2; olive with brown markings

Incubation: 28–32 days; female and male incubate

Fledging: 65 days; female and male feed the young

Migration: complete, to southwestern states, Mexico

Food: insects, fruit, worms, plants, amphibians

Compare: A tall, long-legged gray bird that is not confused with other birds. Look for Sandhill Crane's scarlet red cap to help identify.

Stan's Notes: Usually seen in large undisturbed fields near water. Preens mud into its feathers, staining its plumage rust brown (see insets). Gives a very loud and distinctive rattling call, often heard before the bird is seen. Flight is characteristic, with a faster upstroke, making the wings look like they're flicking in flight. Can fly at heights of over 10,000 feet (3,050 m). Nests on the ground in a large mound of aquatic vegetation. Performs a spectacular mating dance: The birds will face each other, then bow and jump into the air while making loud cackling sounds and flapping their wings. They will also flip sticks and grass into the air during their dance.

male

female

SUMMER

Violet-green Swallow
Tachycineta thalassina

Size: 5¼" (13.5 cm)

Male: Dull emerald green crown, nape and back. Violet-blue wings and tail. White chest and belly. White cheeks with white extending above the eyes. Wings extend beyond the tail when perching.

Female: same as male, only duller

Juvenile: similar to adult of the same sex

Nest: cavity; female and male build nest in tree cavities, old woodpecker holes; 1 brood per year

Eggs: 4–6; pale white with brown markings

Incubation: 13–14 days; female incubates

Fledging: 18–24 days; female and male feed the young

Migration: complete, to Central and South America

Food: insects

Compare: Similar size as the Cliff Swallow (p. 127) which has a distinctive tan-to-rust pattern on the head. Barn Swallow (p. 109) has a distinctive, deeply forked tail.

Stan's Notes: A solitary nester in tree cavities and rarely beneath cliff overhangs. Like Tree Swallows, it can be attracted with a nest box. Will search for miles for errant feathers to line its nest. Tail is short and wing tips extend beyond the end of it, seen when perching. Returns to the state in late April and begins nesting in May. Young often leave the nest by June. On cloudy days they look black but on sunny days they look metallic green.

female
p. 231

male

Mallard
Anas platyrhynchos

YEAR-ROUND
SUMMER
WINTER

Size: 19–21" (48–53 cm)

Male: Large, bulbous green head, white necklace and rust-brown or chestnut chest. Gray-and-white sides. Yellow bill. Orange legs and feet.

Female: brown with an orange-and-black bill and blue-and-white wing mark (speculum)

Juvenile: same as female but with a yellow bill

Nest: ground; female builds; 1 brood per year

Eggs: 7–10; greenish to whitish, unmarked

Incubation: 26–30 days; female incubates

Fledging: 42–52 days; female leads the young to food

Migration: complete to non-migrator in parts of Alaska

Food: seeds, plants, aquatic insects; will come to ground feeders offering corn

Compare: Male Red-breasted Merganser (p. 349) has a shaggy crest and an orange bill. The male Northern Shoveler (p. 347) has a white chest with rust on sides and a dark spoon shaped bill. Male Northern Pintail (p. 241) has long tail feathers and a brown head.

Stan's Notes: A familiar dabbling duck of lakes and ponds. Also found in rivers, streams and some backyards. Tips forward to feed on vegetation on the bottom of shallow water. The name "Mallard" comes from the Latin word *masculus*, meaning "male," referring to the male's habit of taking no part in raising the young. Male and female have white underwings and white tails, but only the male has black central tail feathers that curl upward. Unlike the female, the male doesn't quack. Returns to its birthplace each year.

female
p. 229

male

Northern Shoveler

Anas clypeata

SUMMER

Size: 19–21" (48–53 cm)

Male: Medium-sized duck with an iridescent green head, rust sides, white chest. Extraordinarily large, spoon-shaped bill, almost always held pointed toward the water.

Female: brown and black all over, green wing patch (speculum) and a large spoon-shaped bill

Juvenile: same as female

Nest: ground; female builds; 1 brood per year

Eggs: 9–12; olive without markings

Incubation: 22–25 days; female incubates

Fledging: 30–60 days; female leads the young to food

Migration: complete, to southwestern states, Mexico

Food: aquatic insects, plants

Compare: Similar to male Mallard (p. 345), but the Northern Shoveler has a large, characteristic spoon-shaped bill.

Stan's Notes: One of several species of shovelers. Called "Shoveler" due to the peculiar, shovel-like shape of its bill. Given the common name "Northern" because it is the only species of these ducks in North America. Seen in shallow wetlands, ponds and small lakes in flocks of 5–10 birds. Flocks fly in tight formation. Swims low in water, pointing its large bill toward the water as if it's too heavy to lift. Feeds mainly by filtering tiny aquatic insects and plants from the surface of the water with its bill.

female
p. 251

male

Red-breasted Merganser
Mergus serrator

YEAR-ROUND
SUMMER

Size: 23" (58 cm)

Male: A shaggy green head and crest. Prominent white collar. Rusty breast. Black-and-white body. Long orange bill.

Female: overall brown to gray with a shaggy reddish head and crest, long orange bill

Juvenile: similar to female

Nest: ground; female builds; 1 brood per year

Eggs: 5–10; olive-green without markings

Incubation: 29–30 days; female incubates

Fledging: 55–65 days; female feeds young

Migration: complete to non-migrator in Alaska

Food: fish, aquatic insects

Compare: Smaller than the male Common Merganser (p. 369), which has white sides and breast and lacks a crest.

Stan's Notes: Breeding resident in Alaska. The most widespread of summer mergansers, arriving in April and leaving in October. Most commonly seen along the southeastern Alaska coast, but can also be seen in large inland freshwater lakes. This duck is a very fast flier, clocked at up to 100 miles (161 km) per hour. Frequently seen flying low across the water. Needs a long run for takeoff with wings flapping to get airborne. Serrated bill helps it catch slippery fish. Usually is a silent duck. Male sometimes gives a soft, catlike meow. Female gives a harsh "krrr-croak." Doesn't breed before 2 years of age. The male abandons the female just after eggs are laid. Females often share nests. Breeds across Alaska and northern Canada. The young leave the nest within 24 hours of hatching, never to return.

in flight

female
p. 369

male

Common Merganser
Mergus merganser

Size: 26–28" (66–71 cm)

Male: Long, thin, duck-like bird with a green head and black back. White sides, chest and neck. Long, pointed, orange bill. Often looks black and white in poor light.

Female: same size and shape as the male, with a rust-red head and ragged "hair," gray body, white chest and chin

Juvenile: same as female

Nest: cavity; female lines an old woodpecker hole or a natural cavity; 1 brood per year

Eggs: 9–11; ivory without markings

Incubation: 28–33 days; female incubates

Fledging: 70–80 days; female feeds the young

Migration: complete, to western states and Mexico

Food: small fish, aquatic insects, amphibians

Compare: Male Mallard (p. 345) is smaller and lacks the black back and long pointed bill. Male Red-breasted Merganser (p. 349) is smaller and lacks the white sides and chest.

Stan's Notes: More commonly seen along rivers than lakes. A large, shallow-water diver that feeds on fish in 10–15 feet (3–4.5 m) of water. Bill has a fine, serrated-like edge that helps catch slippery fish. Female often lays some eggs in other merganser nests (egg dumping), resulting in up to 15 young in some broods. Male leaves female once she starts incubating. Orphans are accepted by other merganser mothers with young. Fast flight, often low and close to the water, in groups but not in formation. Usually not vocal except for an alarm call.

SUMMER

Rufous Hummingbird
Selasphorus rufus

Size: 3¾" (9.5 cm)

Male: Tiny burnt-orange bird with a black throat patch (gorget) that reflects orange-red in sunlight. White chest. Green-to-tan flanks.

Female: same as male, but lacking the throat patch

Juvenile: similar to female

Nest: cup; female builds; 1–2 broods per year

Eggs: 1–3; white without markings

Incubation: 14–17 days; female incubates

Fledging: 21–26 days; female feeds young

Migration: complete, to Central and South America

Food: nectar, insects; will come to nectar feeders

Compare: The only regularly occurring hummingbird found in Alaska. Identify it by the unique orange-red (rufous) color.

Stan's Notes: One of the smallest birds in the state. This is a bold, hardy hummer. Frequently seen well out of its normal range in the western U.S., showing up along the East Coast. Visits hummingbird feeders in your yard during migration. Does not sing, but it will chatter or buzz to communicate. Weighing just 2–3 grams, it takes about five average-sized hummingbirds to equal the weight of one chickadee. The heart beats up to an incredible 1,260 times per minute. Male performs a spectacular pendulum-like flight over the perched female. After mating, the female will fly off to build a nest and raise young, without any help from her mate. Constructs a soft, flexible nest that expands to accommodate the growing young.

male

female

YEAR-ROUND
SUMMER

Varied Thrush
Ixoreus naevius

Size: 9½" (24 cm)

Male: Potbellied robin-like bird with orange eyebrows, chin, breast and wing bars. Head, neck and back are gray to blue. Black breast band and eye mark.

Female: browner version of male, lacking the black breast band

Juvenile: similar to female

Nest: cup; female builds; 1–2 broods per year

Eggs: 3–5; pale blue with brown markings

Incubation: 12–14 days; female and male incubate

Fledging: 10–15 days; female and male feed young

Migration: complete to non-migrator, to western states

Food: insects, fruit

Compare: Similar size and shape as American Robin (p. 299), but the Varied Thrush has a warm-orange breast unlike the red breast of Robin. Male Thrush has a distinctive black breast band.

Stan's Notes: This intriguing-looking bird nests in the southern two-thirds of Alaska. Prefers moist coniferous forests. It is most common in dense, older coniferous forests in high elevations. In the Lower 48 States, it migrates in an east-west pattern. Some birds in western states fly eastward in fall, showing up in nearly any state. Usually is very elusive, feeding on the ground in dense vegetation. Tosses leaves around in search of fallen berries and insects. Gives a distinctive song of long whistles, repeated after a short pause.

male

female
p. 405

YEAR-ROUND

Red Crossbill
Loxia curvirostra

Size: 6½" (16 cm)

Male: Sparrow-sized bird, dirty-red to orange with bright-red crown and rump. Long, pointed, crossed bill. Dark-brown wings and a short dark-brown tail.

Female: pale-yellow chest, light-gray throat patch, a crossed bill, dark-brown wings and tail

Juvenile: streaked with tinges of yellow, bill gradually crosses about 2 weeks after fledging

Nest: cup; female builds; 1 brood per year

Eggs: 3–4; bluish white with brown markings

Incubation: 14–18 days; female incubates

Fledging: 16–20 days; female and male feed young

Migration: irruptive; moves around Alaska in winter to find food, will wander as far as Mexico

Food: seeds, leaf buds; comes to seed feeders

Compare: The male White-winged Crossbill (p. 359) has white wing bars. Male Pine Grosbeak (p. 361) lacks the crossed bill.

Stan's Notes: The long crossed bill is adapted for extracting seeds from pine and spruce cones, its favorite food. Often dangles upside down like a parrot to reach cones. Also seen on the ground where it eats grit, which helps digest food. Nests in coniferous forests at any elevation, mainly west of the Cascades. Plumage can be highly variable among individuals. While it is a resident nester, migrating crossbills from farther north move into the state during winter, searching for food, swelling populations. This irruptive behavior makes it more common in some winters and nonexistent in others.

female
p. 407

male

White-winged Crossbill
Loxia leucoptera

Size: 6½" (16 cm)

Male: Red-to-pink sparrow-sized bird with black wings and tail. Two large white wing bars. Gray sides and lower belly. A long, slender crossed bill with a dark spot at base (lore).

Female: pale yellow breast with indistinct streaks, dark wings, 2 large white wing bars, dark tail, a long, slender crossed bill

Juvenile: similar to female, the first-year male is pale yellow or pale red

Nest: cup; female builds; 1 brood per year

Eggs: 3–5; pale blue with brown markings

Incubation: 12–14 days; female incubates

Fledging: 16–20 days; female and male feed young

Migration: non-migrator to irruptive; moves around in winter to find food

Food: seeds, berries, insects; comes to seed feeders

Compare: The male Red Crossbill (p. 357) is very similar to the male White-winged Crossbill, but lacks white wing bars. Male Pine Grosbeak (p. 361) is much larger and lacks the crossed bill.

Stan's Notes: This bird dangles upside down to reach pine and spruce cones, using its long crossed bill to extracts the seeds. Eats berries and insects to a lesser extent. Usually seen on the ground picking up grit, which helps grind the seeds. Moves around to find a plentiful supply of seeds. Plumage can be highly variable among individuals, with older males more colorful than the younger ones.

female
p. 297

male

Pine Grosbeak
Pinicola enucleator

**YEAR-ROUND
SUMMER**

Size: 9" (23 cm)

Male: Plump rose-and-gray finch with a long dark tail. Dark wings smattered with gray. Two white wing bars. Short, pointed dark bill.

Female: mostly gray with dark wings and tail, head and rump have a dull-yellow tinge

Juvenile: male has a touch of red on head and rump; female is similar to the adult female

Nest: cup; female builds; 1 brood per year

Eggs: 4–5; bluish-green without markings

Incubation: 13–15 days; female incubates

Fledging: 13–20 days; female and male feed the young

Migration: partial to non-migrator to irruptive; moves around in winter to find food

Food: seeds, fruit, insects; will come to seed feeders

Compare: The male Red Crossbill (p. 357) and male White-winged Crossbill (p. 359) are much smaller and have a crossed bill.

Stan's Notes: This finch is common in Alaska in some years and not so common in others. A very tame and approachable seed eater. Often seen along roads or on the ground, eating tiny grains of sand and dirt, which help aid digestion. Favors coniferous woods, rarely moving out of coniferous regions during summer, but also likes mixed forests. Will bathe in fluffy snow. Flies in a typical finch-like undulating pattern while giving soft, whistle "cheer" calls. Male sings a rich, beautiful song all year long. Male and female develop a pouch in the bottom of their mouths (buccal pouch) during the breeding season for transporting seeds to their young.

nonbreeding
p. 309

breeding

SUMMER MIGRATION

Red Knot
Calidris canutus

Size: 11" (28 cm)

Male: Breeding (May–Aug) has a salmon-colored head, chest and belly Gray-to-brown back and wings. Medium straight black bill.

Female: same as male

Juvenile: overall gray with white eyebrows and dull yellow legs

Nest: ground; male and female construct; 1 brood per year

Eggs: 3–4; olive with brown markings

Incubation: 21–23 days; male and female incubate

Fledging: 18–20 days; female and male feed young

Migration: complete, to coastal California, Mexico and Central and South America

Food: insects, mollusks, snails, marine worms, small fish

Compare: Breeding Western Sandpiper (p. 143) has a rusty brown back and a white belly The breeding Dunlin (p. 159) has a large black patch on belly. The Whimbrel (p. 213) has a much longer bill and lacks a reddish belly.

Stan's Notes: One of the longest migrating shorebirds, nesting on the Arctic tundra and wintering as far south as Tierra del Fuego, Argentina. Stops in coastal North America. Feeds in large flocks of up to 100 individuals, often with other shorebirds. Usually is seen standing on one leg on the beach, resting between feedings. Was the most abundant shorebird in North America; hunting in the late 1800s to early 1900s severely reduced the overall population.

female p. 227

male

Redhead
Aythya americana

SUMMER

Size: 19" (48 cm)

Male: Rich-red head and neck with a black breast and tail, gray sides, and smoky-gray wings and back. Tricolored bill with a light-blue base, white ring and black tip.

Female: soft-brown, plain-looking duck with gray-to-white wing linings, a rounded top of head and a gray bill with a black tip

Juvenile: similar to female

Nest: cup; female builds; 1 brood per year

Eggs: 9–14; white without markings

Incubation: 24–28 days; female and male incubate

Fledging: 56–73 days; female shows young what to eat

Migration: complete migrator, to southwestern states, Mexico and Central America

Food: seeds, aquatic plants, insects

Compare: The male Northern Shoveler (p. 347) has a green head and rusty sides, unlike the red head and gray sides of the male Redhead.

Stan's Notes: A duck of permanent large bodies of water. Forages along the shoreline, feeding on seeds, aquatic plants and insects. Usually builds nest directly on the water's surface, using large mats of vegetation. Female lays up to 75 percent of its eggs in the nests of other Redheads and several other duck species. Nests primarily in the Prairie Pothole region of the northern Great Plains. The overall populations seem to be increasing at about 2–3 percent each year.

female
p. 239

male

SUMMER

Canvasback
Aythya valisineria

Size: 20–21" (51–53 cm)

Male: Deep-red head with a sloping forehead that transitions into a long black bill. Red neck. Gray-and-white sides and back. Black chest and tail.

Female: similar to male, but has a brown head, neck and chest, light gray-to-brown sides and a long dark bill

Juvenile: similar to female

Nest: ground; female builds; 1 brood per year

Eggs: 7–9; pale white to gray without markings

Incubation: 24–29 days; female incubates

Fledging: 56–67 days; female leads young to food

Migration: complete, to western coastal states, Mexico

Food: aquatic insects, small clams

Compare: The male Greater Scaup (p. 85) and male Lesser Scaup (p. 73) are smaller, lack the red head and neck of the male Canvasback and have a shorter, light blue bill.

Stan's Notes: A large inland duck of freshwater lakes, rivers and ponds. Populations declined dramatically in the 1960–80s due to marsh drainage for agriculture. Females return to their birthplace (philopatric) while males disperse to new areas. Will mate during migration or on the breeding grounds. A courting male gives a soft cooing call when displaying and during aerial chases. Male leaves the female after incubation starts. Female takes a new mate every year. Female feeds very little during incubation and will lose up to 70 percent of fat reserves during that time.

in flight

male
p. 351

female

Common Merganser
Mergus merganser

SUMMER

Size: 26–28" (66–71 cm)

Female: Long, thin, duck-like bird with a rust-red head and ragged "hair." Gray body and white chest and chin. Long, pointed, orange bill.

Male: same size and shape as the female, but with a green head, a black back and white sides

Juvenile: same as female

Nest: cavity; female lines an old woodpecker hole or a natural cavity; 1 brood per year

Eggs: 9–11; ivory without markings

Incubation: 28–33 days; female incubates

Fledging: 70–80 days; female feeds the young

Migration: complete, to western states and Mexico

Food: small fish, aquatic insects

Compare: Female Red-breasted Merganser (p. 251) is smaller with a smaller, thinner bill. Look for ragged "hair" on head, a long, pointed orange bill and white chest and chin.

Stan's Notes: More commonly seen along rivers than lakes. A large, shallow-water diver that feeds on fish in 10–15 feet (3–4.5 m) of water. Bill has a fine, serrated-like edge that helps catch slippery fish. The female often lays some eggs in other merganser nests (egg dumping), resulting in up to 15 young in some broods. Male leaves the female once she starts incubating. Orphans are accepted by other merganser mothers with young. Fast flight, often low and close to the water, in groups but not in formation. Usually not vocal except for an alarm call that sounds like a muffled quack.

juvenile

in flight

SUMMER

Arctic Tern
Sterna paradisaea

Size: 12" (30 cm)

Male: A white and gray tern with a black cap and small dark red bill. Short red legs. Forked tail, seen in flight. Nonbreeding plumage has an incomplete black cap and black bill.

Female: same as male

Juvenile: similar to nonbreeding plumage, scattered brown overall

Nest: ground; female and male construct; 1 brood per year

Eggs: 2; olive with brown markings

Incubation: 20–24 days; female and male incubate

Fledging: 21–28 days; male and female feed young

Migration: complete, to South America

Food: small fish, aquatic insects, insects

Compare: Smaller than the breeding Bonaparte's Gull (p. 379), which has a black head, black tail and tips of wings. Look for Arctic Terns forked tail to help identify in flight.

Stan's Notes: Catches small fish by diving headfirst in water. Nests in large colonies with other tern species. While most nesting occurs in Alaska and the Northwest Territories of Canada, it also nests as far south as Maine. Returns to same nest site every year. Vigorously defends nest site and young from predators and people. Long-term relationship between mates. Young remain with the adults during migration to South America.

breeding
p. 183

winter

White-tailed ptarmigan
Lagopus leucura

YEAR-ROUND

Size: 12½" (32 cm)

Male: Winter plumage (Oct–Apr) is entirely white. Small dark bill.

Female: same as winter male

Juvenile: similar to breeding female, white on wings

Nest: ground; female builds; 1 brood per year

Eggs: 4–8; tan with brown markings

Incubation: 22–24 days; female incubates

Fledging: 10–15 days; female shows young what to eat

Migration: non-migrator to partial; will move around in winter to find food

Food: leaf and flower buds, seeds, insects, berries

Compare: The winter Willow Ptarmigan (p. 377) has black sides on its tail. The winter male Rock Ptarmigan (p. 375) has a black eye line.

Stan's Notes: Alone or in small unisex flocks in winter. Ptarmigans molt three times each year; other birds molt twice. In late autumn, molts to an all-white plumage that blends with winter landscapes. Moves to lower elevations during winter. Late summer plumage (Jul–Oct) is gray with rust and black spotting. When courting, male displays swollen red combs and alternates the pace of strutting, fast with slow. Female builds a shallow nest in spring, usually under a shrub, and lines it with fine grass, lichens and feathers. She delays nesting until fully molted into her summer camouflage plumage. If threatened at the nest, the female will perform a distraction display that includes hissing and clucking. Male leaves female shortly after eggs hatch. Species name *leucura* is Greek and means "white tail." Other ptarmigans have black-sided tails.

winter

breeding
p. 185

Rock Ptarmigan
Lagopus muta

YEAR-ROUND

Size: 14" (36 cm)

Male: Winter (Oct–Apr) is all white except for a black eye line and a black-sided tail, seen in flight. Small dark bill.

Female: all white, small dark bill, lacks eye lines

Juvenile: similar to breeding female, white outermost flight feathers

Nest: ground; female builds; 1 brood per year

Eggs: 6–9; tan with brown markings

Incubation: 21–24 days; female incubates

Fledging: 12–20 days; female shows young what to eat

Migration: non-migrator to partial; will move around in winter to find food

Food: leaf and flower buds, seeds, insects, berries

Compare: The winter Willow Ptarmigan (p. 377) has a thicker bill than the winter female Rock Ptarmigan. Winter White-tailed Ptarmigan (p. 373) lacks eye lines and black on tail.

Stan's Notes: Solitary or in small unisex flocks in winter. All ptarmigans molt three times each year; most other birds molt twice. Molts in late autumn to white plumage and blends into winter landscapes. Molts in late winter into breeding plumage. Courting male (Apr–Jun) is mostly white with bright red combs and a dirty yellow and tan chest. Male displays his red combs to female. Female builds a shallow ground nest, often among rocks, and covers it with vegetation until clutch is complete. Common name comes from its habitat on rocky tundra. Latin species name *muta* means "animal that can only mutter or has a weak call" and refers to its quiet call.

breeding
p. 187

winter

Willow Ptarmigan
Lagopus lagopus

YEAR-ROUND

Size: 14" (36 cm)

Male: Winter plumage (Oct–Apr) is entirely white with a stout black bill. Black edges on tail, seen in flight.

Female: same as winter male

Juvenile: similar to breeding female, white on wings

Nest: ground; female builds; 1 brood per year

Eggs: 5–14; blackish brown with cream markings

Incubation: 21–23 days; female incubates

Fledging: 10–14 days; female shows young what to eat

Migration: non-migrator to partial; will move around in winter to find food

Food: buds (mainly willow), seeds, insects

Compare: Winter White-tailed Ptarmigan (p. 373) lacks black edges on tail. The winter male Rock Ptarmigan (p. 375) has a black stripe through its eyes.

Stan's Notes: "Ptarmigan" comes from a Gaelic word for this kind, of bird, *tarmachan*. Common name comes from its favor for willow buds and leaves. All ptarmigans molt three times each year; most , other birds molt twice. Molts to white plumage in late autumn that blends in with the winter landscape. Moves to lower elevations in winter. During spring, female molts to a camouflage coloration that enables her to blend in with landscape while she incubates. Builds nest on the open tundra; lines its nest with leaves, grass and a few feathers. Unlike other ptarmigan species, the male remains with the female to raise young. However, females without mates are just as successful rearing their young as the females with mates.

in flight

breeding

winter

Bonaparte's Gull

Chroicocephalus philadelphia

Size: 13½" (34.5 cm); up to 3' wingspan

Male: Mostly white during breeding season (Apr–Aug) with gray upper surface of wings and back. Black head, small black bill and white crescent marks around eyes. Black tips of wings and tail, seen in flight. Winter lacks a black head and has a dark ear spot.

Female: same as male

Juvenile: similar to winter male

Nest: platform; female and male construct; 1–2 broods per year

Eggs: 2–4; light brown with brown markings

Incubation: 20–24 days; female and male incubate

Fledging: 21–25 days; female and male feed young

Migration: complete, to coastal California and Mexico

Food: aquatic and terrestrial insects, fish

Compare: Larger than Arctic Tern (p. 371), which has a black cap unlike the black head of the breeding Bonaparte's Gull. Look for a small black bill to help identify Bonaparte's Gull.

Stan's Notes: Rarely with other gull species, presumably due to its small size. Rarely found away from the coast during winter, but on lakes and rivers during migration. Said to resemble a tern species due to its small size, short thin bill and swift flight. Nests in half of Alaska where there is water. Builds its own nest or takes an abandoned nest in a tree, mainly conifers. Takes two years for young to obtain adult plumage.

in flight

breeding

winter

Short-billed Gull

Larus brachyrhynchus

Size: 16" (40 cm); up to 3½' wingspan

Male: White gull with dark-gray back and wings. Black wing tips. Red ring around dark eyes. Yellow legs. Breeding has a small unmarked yellow bill. Winter plumage has a brown-streaked head and neck. Yellow bill with a dark ring around the tip.

Female: same as male

Juvenile: gray to brown overall with a black-tipped yellow bill

Nest: ground; female and male construct; 1 brood per year

Eggs: 2–3; brown with brown markings

Incubation: 24–26 days; female and male incubate

Fledging: 30–32 days; female and male feed young

Migration: non-migrator to complete, to western coastal U.S. and Mexico

Food: insects, fish, shellfish, fruit

Compare: Herring Gull (p. 385) and Glaucous-winged Gull (p. 387) are much larger. Look for the tiny yellow bill and diminutive size.

Stan's Notes: Small gull with a remarkably small bill. A common summer resident in most of Alaska. Often drops sea urchins from heights to crack open and eat. This is a three-year gull, taking three years to reach maturity. Starts out entirely light brown. With a brown-streaked head and neck, the second-year gull resembles the winter adult. Third-year gull has breeding plumage. Doesn't nest in the state, nesting in northwestern Canada and Alaska instead. The young return to their natal colony to nest.

male

female

YEAR-ROUND
WINTER

Snowy Owl
Bubo scandiacus

Size: 23" (58 cm); up to 4' wingspan

Male: All white with a relatively small round head, bright yellow eyes and small dark bill. Feet are completely covered with white feathers.

Female: same as male, but dark bars overall

Juvenile: gray with a white face (gray changes later to white), covered with dark horizontal bars, the younger the bird, the more barring

Nest: ground, often in gravel or atop a hummock; 1 brood per year

Eggs: 3–4; white without markings

Incubation: 32–34 days; female incubates

Fledging: 14–20 days; male and female feed young

Migration: partial to non-migrator, irruptive, to Alaska, Canada and northern states

Food: mammals, birds

Compare: Our only white owl, rarely confused with any other bird.

Stan's Notes: A nesting bird in parts of coastal Alaska, known for feeding on lemmings. Moves down through the state in winter in search of food when lemmings aren't plentiful. In some years, may move as far south as northern Texas. The clutch size is dependent on the availability of prey. Prefers to rest on the ground. Male feeds incubating female, but does not incubate. Young hatch several days apart (asynchronously). Families remain together until fall. Often seen on frozen lakes or bays in winter. Blends in with snow. Flies low to the ground on relatively narrow wings with full, stiff wing beats. Shy and unapproachable, unlike many other owls.

in flight

breeding

juvenile

winter

Herring Gull
Larus argentatus

YEAR-ROUND
SUMMER
MIGRATION
WINTER

Size: 23–26" (58–66 cm); up to 5' wingspan

Male: White with slate-gray wings. Black wing tips with tiny white spots. Yellow bill with an orange-red spot near the tip of the lower bill (mandible). Pinkish legs and feet. Winter plumage has gray speckles on head and neck.

Female: same as male

Juvenile: mottled brown to gray, with a black bill

Nest: ground; female and male construct; 1 brood per year

Eggs: 2–3; olive with brown markings

Incubation: 24–28 days; female and male incubate

Fledging: 35–36 days; female and male feed the young

Migration: complete, to southern coastal Alaska, western states and Mexico; non-migrator in parts of Alaska

Food: fish, insects, clams, eggs, baby birds

Compare: Glaucous-winged Gull (p. 387) is similar, but has gray wing tips with white spots. Glaucous Gull (p. 389) is also similar, but has unmarked white wing tips.

Stan's Notes: A common gull of large lakes. An opportunistic bird, scavenging for human food in dumpsters, parking lots and other places with garbage. Takes eggs and young from other bird nests. Often drops clams and other shellfish from heights to break the shells and get to the soft interior. Nests in colonies, returning to the same site annually. Lines its nest with grass and seaweed. It takes about four years for the juveniles to obtain adult plumage. Adults have spotted heads during winter.

nonbreeding
in flight

breeding
in flight

winter

juvenile

juvenile
in flight

YEAR-ROUND
SUMMER

Glaucous-winged Gull
Larus glaucescens

Size: 26" (66 cm); up to 4¾' wingspan

Male: White gull with a light-gray back and wings, with white spots on wing tips. Yellow bill with red spot on the lower bill. Dark eyes with a pink eye-ring around each eye. Pink legs. Winter plumage has a brown-streaked head and neck.

Female: same as male

Juvenile: gray to brown overall with a black bill

Nest: ground; female and male construct; 1 brood per year

Eggs: 1–3; olive with brown markings

Incubation: 27–29 days; female and male incubate

Fledging: 35–55 days; female and male feed young

Migration: partial to non-migrator in Alaska

Food: insects, fish, shellfish, garbage

Compare: Glaucous Gull (p. 389) is nearly identical, but has a yellow eye-ring around each eye and unmarked white wing tips.

Stan's Notes: A four-year gull, taking four years to reach maturity. Starts out entirely gray to brown. Second-year gull is light gray with patches of white. Third-year gull resembles the winter adult, with a brown-streaked head and neck, white body and gray back and wings. Fourth-year gull has breeding plumage. Returns to the same nesting colony each year, often breeding with mate from previous year. Male bends forward and pops head up while calling for mate. Hybridizes with Glaucous Gulls and Herring Gulls.

in flight

breeding

winter

Glaucous Gull
Larus hyperboreus

YEAR-ROUND
SUMMER
WINTER

Size: 27" (69 cm); up to 5' wingspan

Male: Breeding (Mar–Sep) plumage is white with a light gray back and upper surface of wings. Unmarked white wing tips. Yellow eye-ring around each eye. Yellow bill with a red spot on lower bill. Winter (Sep–Apr) has brown streaks on head and nape.

Female: same as male

Juvenile: overall light brown with a black-tipped bill

Nest: ground; female and male construct; 1 brood per year

Eggs: 2–4; olive with brown markings

Incubation: 27–28 days; female and male incubate

Fledging: 45–50 days; female and male feed young

Migration: complete to non-migrator, to the southern coast of Alaska

Food: small fish, aquatic insects, carrion, bird eggs

Compare: Nearly identical to Glaucous-winged Gull (p. 387), which has gray wing tips with white spots and pink eye-rings.

Stan's Notes: One of the largest and palest of our gulls. A four-year gull that starts out light brown with a black-tipped bill. Second year gull is nearly all white. Third-year gull has a gray back and upper wing surface with brown streaks on head and nape of neck. Attains breeding plumage in the fourth year. Nests in large colonies, often with other species, on rocky coasts, islands and tundra lakes. Constructs a large mound of soft grass and other plant material and usually lines it with feathers. Uses the same nest for many years.

blue morph

juvenile

white
morph

in flight

Snow Goose
Chen caerulescens

SUMMER MIGRATION

Size: 25–38" (64–97 cm); up to 4½' wingspan

Male: White morph has black wing tips and varying patches of black and brown. Blue morph has a white head and a gray breast and back. Both morphs have a pink bill and legs.

Female: same as male

Juvenile: overall dull gray with a dark bill

Nest: ground; female builds; 1 brood per year

Eggs: 3–5; white without markings

Incubation: 23–25 days; female incubates

Fledging: 45–49 days; female and male teach the young to feed

Migration: complete, to southwestern states, Mexico

Food: aquatic insects and plants

Compare: The Tundra Swan (p. 393) and Trumpeter Swan (p. 395) lack black wing tips. The Canada Goose (p. 339) has a black neck and white chin strap.

Stan's Notes: This bird occurs in light (white) and dark (blue) color morphs. The white morph is more common than the blue. A bird of wide-open fields, wetlands and lakes of any size. It has a thick, serrated bill, which helps it to grab and pull up plants. Breeds in large colonies on the northern tundra in Canada. Female starts to breed at 2–3 years. Older females produce more eggs and are more successful at reproduction than younger females. Seen by the thousands during migration and in winter. Commonly seen with Sandhill Cranes. Has a classic goose-like call.

juvenile

in flight

SUMMER
MIGRATION

Tundra Swan
Cygnus columbianus

Size: 50–54" (127–137 cm); up to 5½' wingspan

Male: Large all-white swan. Black bill, legs and feet. Small yellow mark in front of each eye.

Female: same as male

Juvenile: same size as adult with gray plumage, pinkish-gray bill

Nest: ground; female and male construct; 1 brood per year

Eggs: 4–5; creamy white without markings

Incubation: 35–40 days; female and male incubate

Fledging: 60–70 days; female and male feed the young

Migration: complete, to West and East Coast states

Food: plants, aquatic insects

Compare: Trumpeter Swan (p. 395) is larger and lacks yellow marks on its face. Snow Goose (p. 391) is much smaller and has black wing tips. Look for Tundra Swans black bill and legs.

Stan's Notes: Nests on the tundra of Alaska, hence its common name. Migrates diagonally across North America to reach wintering grounds on the East Coast. Flies in large V-shaped wedges. Gathers in large numbers of several thousand during the winter. Often seen in large family groups of 20 or more individuals. Gives a high-pitched, whistle-like call. Young are easy to distinguish by their gray plumage and pinkish bills.

in flight

juvenile

Trumpeter Swan
Cygnus buccinator

YEAR-ROUND
MIGRATION

Size: 58–62" (147–157 cm); up to 6½' wingspan

Male: A large all-white swan with an all-black bill, legs and feet.

Female: same as male

Juvenile: same size as adult, with gray plumage and a pinkish-gray bill

Nest: ground; female and male construct; 1 brood per year

Eggs: 4–6; cream-white without markings

Incubation: 33–37 days; female incubates

Fledging: 100–120 days; female and male show the young what to eat

Migration: complete, to coastal Canada and West Coast states; non-migrator where it can find open water

Food: aquatic plants, insects

Compare: The Tundra Swan (p. 393) is very similar, but it has small yellow marks in front of its eyes (lores). Snow Goose (p. 391) is much smaller and has black wing tips.

Stan's Notes: Was once eliminated from both states due to market hunting, but reintroduced with great success. Reintroduced birds are identified by large colored tags on the neck or wings. Most breeding programs were started with eggs taken from Trumpeters in Alaska. Often on larger rivers. Also in wetlands, marshes, small lakes, ponds and farm fields. Mated pairs defend large territories and construct large mound nests at the edge of water. Named for its loud, trumpet-like call, typically given in flight.

female

male

SUMMER

Wilson's Warbler
Cardellina pusilla

Size: 4¾" (12 cm)

Male: Dull-yellow upper and bright-yellow lower. Distinctive black cap. Large black eyes and small thin bill.

Female: same as male, but lacking the black cap

Juvenile: similar to female

Nest: cup; female builds; 1 brood per year

Eggs: 4–6; white with brown markings

Incubation: 10–13 days; female incubates

Fledging: 8–11 days; female and male feed young

Migration: complete, to coastal Texas, Mexico and Central America

Food: insects

Compare: The Orange-crowned Warbler (p. 399) is paler yellow and lacks the black cap of the male Wilson's Warbler. The Eastern Yellow Wagtail (p. 403) is larger, has white eye brows and lacks male Wilson's black cap.

Stan's Notes: A widespread warbler of low to mid-level elevations. Can be found near water in willow and alder thickets. Its all-insect diet makes it one of the top insect-eating birds in North America. Often flicks its tail and spreads its wings when hopping among thick shrubs, looking for insects. Females often mate with males that have the best territories and that might already have mates (polygyny).

SUMMER

Orange-crowned Warbler
Leiothlypis celata

Size: 5" (13 cm)

Male: An overall pale-yellow bird with a dark line through eyes. Faint streaking on sides and chest. Tawny-orange crown, often invisible. Small thin bill.

Female: same as male, but very slightly duller, often indistinguishable in the field

Juvenile: same as adults

Nest: cup; female builds; 1–2 broods per year

Eggs: 3–6; white with brown markings

Incubation: 12–14 days; female incubates

Fledging: 8–10 days; female and male feed young

Migration: complete, to coastal California, Mexico and Central America

Food: insects, fruit, nectar

Compare: Male Wilson's Warbler (p. 397) is brighter yellow with a distinctive black cap. Yellow Warbler (p. 401) is darker yellow than the pale yellow of the Orange-crowned.

Stan's Notes: A nesting resident in most of Alaska but often seen more during migration when large groups move together. Builds a bulky, well-concealed nest on the ground with nest rim at ground level. Known to feed at sapsucker taps and drink flower nectar. The orange crown tends to be hidden and is rarely seen in the field. A widespread breeder, from western Texas to Alaska and across Canada and south to California.

male

female

Yellow Warbler
Setophaga petechia

Size: 5" (13 cm)

Male: Yellow with thin orange streaks on the chest and belly. Long, pointed dark bill.

Female: same as male but lacks orange streaks

Juvenile: similar to female but much duller

Nest: cup; female builds; 1 brood per year

Eggs: 4–5; white with brown markings

Incubation: 11–12 days; female incubates

Fledging: 10–12 days; female and male feed the young

Migration: complete, to southwestern states, Mexico, and Central and South America

Food: insects

Compare: Look for the orange streaking on the chest of the male. The Orange-crowned Warbler (p. 399) is paler yellow. Yellow-rumped Warbler (p. 273) has only spots of yellow unlike the orange streaking on the chest of the male Yellow Warbler.

Stan's Notes: A common warbler throughout most of Alaska. Seen in gardens and shrubby areas close to water. A prolific insect eater, gleaning caterpillars and other insects from tree leaves. Male sings a string of notes that sound like "sweet, sweet, sweet, I'm-so-sweet!" Begins to migrate south in August. Returns in late April. Males arrive in spring before females to claim territories. Migrates at night in mixed flocks of warblers. Rests and feeds during the day.

Eastern Yellow Wagtail
Motacilla tschutschensis

Size: 6½" (16 cm)

Male: Yellow chest and belly. Head and back are dull yellow to olive green. White chin. Dark cheek patches. Narrow white eyebrows.

Female: similar to male

Juvenile: overall gray with a dark border around a white throat

Nest: cup; female builds; 1 brood per year

Eggs: 4–7; pale white with brown markings

Incubation: 10–14 days; female and male incubate

Fledging: 14–16 days; female and male feed young

Migration: complete, to the East Indies, China, Asia and southern North Africa

Food: insects, snails, berries, worms

Compare: Larger than the male Northern Wheatear (p. 277), which has a black mask and wings. Male Wilson's Warbler (p. 397) is smaller, has a black cap and lacks the white eyebrows of Eastern Yellow Wagtail.

Stan's Notes: Named for the continuous up and down motion of its tail. Nests beneath an overhanging bank or next to a clump of plants (tussock). Builds nest from grass and leaves and lines it with hair and feathers. Male performs a courtship flight of up to 90 feet (27 m) and floats down on stiff cupped wing, singing slowly while spreading and elevating its tail. When close to ground, it glides to a perch or lands on the ground, then repeats flight and display. In North America, it is found only in Alaska. Migrates west to Eurasia, where it is widespread and very common.

male
p. 357

female

Red Crossbill
Loxia curvirostra

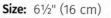

YEAR-ROUND

Size: 6½" (16 cm)

Female: A pale yellow-gray sparrow-sized bird with a pale-yellow chest and light-gray patch on the throat. Long, pointed, crossed bill. Dark-brown wings and a short dark-brown tail.

Male: dirty red to orange with a bright-red crown and rump, a crossed bill, dark-brown wings and a short dark-brown tail

Juvenile: streaked with tinges of yellow, bill gradually crosses about 2 weeks after fledging

Nest: cup; female builds; 1 brood per year

Eggs: 3–4; bluish white with brown markings

Incubation: 14–18 days; female incubates

Fledging: 16–20 days; female and male feed young

Migration: irruptive; moves around Alaska in winter to find food, will wander as far as Mexico

Food: seeds, leaf buds; comes to seed feeders

Compare: Female White-winged Crossbill (p. 407) has white wing bars. Female Pine Grosbeak (p. 297) lacks the crossed bill.

Stan's Notes: The long crossed bill is adapted for extracting seeds from pine and spruce cones, its favorite food. Often dangles upside down like a parrot to reach cones. Also seen on the ground where it eats grit, which helps digest food. Nests in coniferous forests. Plumage can be highly variable among individuals. Some studies show up to nine distinct populations of Red Crossbills, but they are nearly impossible to distinguish in the field. Irruptive behavior makes it more common in some winters and nonexistent in others.

male
p. 359

female

White-winged Crossbill
Loxia leucoptera

YEAR-ROUND

Size: 6½" (16 cm)

Female: Sparrow-sized bird with a pale yellow breast covered with indistinct streaks. Dark wings. Two large white wing bars. Dark tail. Long, slender crossed bill.

Male: red-to-pink bird, black wings and tail, 2 large white wing bars, gray sides and lower belly, a long, slender crossed bill with a dark spot at base (lore)

Juvenile: similar to female

Nest: cup; female builds; 1 brood per year

Eggs: 3–5; pale blue with brown markings

Incubation: 12–14 days; female incubates

Fledging: 16–20 days; female and male feed young

Migration: non-migrator to irruptive; moves around in winter to find food

Food: seeds, berries, insects; comes to seed feeders

Compare: The female Red Crossbill (p. 405) is very similar to female White-winged Crossbill, but lacks the white wing bars. The female Pine Grosbeak (p. 297) is much larger and lacks the crossed bill.

Stan's Notes: This bird dangles upside down to reach pine and spruce cones, using its long crossed bill to extracts the seeds. Eats berries and insects to a lesser extent. Usually seen on the ground picking up grit, which helps grind the seeds. Moves around to find a plentiful supply of seeds. Plumage can be highly variable among individuals, with older males more colorful than the younger ones.

BIRDING ON THE INTERNET

Birding online is a great way to discover additional information and learn more about birds. These websites will assist you in your pursuit of birds. Web addresses sometimes change a bit, so if one no longer works, just enter the name of the group into a search engine to track down the new address.

Site	Address
Author Stan Tekiela's homepage	naturesmart.com
Alaska Raptor Center	alaskaraptor.org
American Birding Association	aba.org
Arctic Audubon Society	www.arcticaudubon.org
Audubon Alaska	ak.audubon.org
The Cornell Lab of Ornithology	birds.cornell.edu
eBird	ebird.org
Juneau Raptor Center	www.juneauraptorcenter.org

CHECKLIST/INDEX BY SPECIES

Use the boxes to check the birds you've seen.

MORE FOR ALASKA BY STAN TEKIELA

Identification Guides

Birds of Prey of the West Field Guide

Birds of the Northwest

Pacific Northwest Birding Companion

Stan Tekiela's Birding for Beginners: Pacific Northwest

Children's Books: Adventure Board Book Series

Floppers & Loppers

Paws & Claws

Peepers & Peekers

Snouts & Sniffers

Children's Books

C is for Cardinal

Can You Count the Critters?

Critter Litter

Children's Books: Wildlife Picture Books

Baby Bear Discovers the World

The Cutest Critter

Do Beavers Need Blankets?

Hidden Critters

Some Babies Are Wild

Super Animal Powers

What Eats That?

Whose Baby Butt?

Whose Butt?

Whose House Is That?

Whose Track Is That?

Nature Books

Bird Trivia

Start Mushrooming

A Year in Nature with Stan Tekiela

Backyard Bird Feeding Guides
Attracting & Feeding Bluebirds
Attracting & Feeding Cardinals
Attracting & Feeding Finches
Attracting & Feeding Hummingbirds
Attracting & Feeding Orioles
Attracting & Feeding Woodpeckers

Favorite Wildlife Series
Bald Eagles
Hummingbirds
Loons
Owls
Wolves, Coyotes & Foxes

Nature Appreciation Series
Bird Nests
Feathers
Wildflowers

Our Love of Wildlife Series
Our Love of Loons
Our Love of Owls

Nature's Wild Cards (playing cards)
Bears
Birds of the Northwest
Hummingbirds
Loons
Mammals of the Northwest
Owls
Raptors
Trees of the Northwest

Wildlife Appreciation Series
Backyard Birds
Bears
Bird Migration
Cranes, Herons & Egrets
Deer, Elk & Moose
Wild Birds

OBSERVATION NOTES